THROUGH THE *Storm*

"Medications" for Your Soul

A Little Book of Prayers, Scriptures, & Meditations

By
REV. BETTY A. BEACH-CONNELL

Copyright © 2016 by Rev. Betty A. Beach-Connell

Through The Storm
"Medications" for Your Soul
by Rev. Betty A. Beach-Connell

Printed in the United States of America.

ISBN 9781498478670

All rights reserved solely by the author. The author guarantees all contents are original and do not infringe upon the legal rights of any other person or work. No part of this book may be reproduced in any form without the permission of the author. The views expressed in this book are not necessarily those of the publisher.

Scripture quotations taken from the New Revised Standard Version (NRSV). Copyright © 1989 World Bible Publishers, Inc. Alsoby Tyndale House Publishers, Inc.

Scripture quotations taken from the Modern English Version (MEV). Copyright © 2014 by Charisma House.

Scripture quotations taken from the New Living Translation (NLT). Copyright © 1996, 2004, 2007 by Tyndale House Foundation. Used by permission. All rights reserved.

www.xulonpress.com

To Luann

You can make your plans but God will direct your steps. Proverbs 16:9

Remember God loves you.

Rev. Betty A Beach-Cornell

Forgive me Lord, for what I've done wrong. I humble myself before You as I give You thanks for forgiving me—You gave up Your life so that I may live.

God grant me the wisdom to come to You daily, seeking forgiveness for going against Your Will and to offer thanksgiving for Your mercy and grace. Grant me guidance, through the power of Your Holy Spirit, in the days to come.

INTRODUCTION

---❄︎---

I pray that your hearts will be flooded with light so that you can understand the confident hope he has given to those he called—his holy people who are his rich and glorious inheritance. I also pray that you will understand the incredible greatness of God's power for those who believe him. This is the same mighty power that raised Christ from the dead and seated him in the place of honor at God's right hand in the heavenly realms.

Based on Ephesians 1:18-20

I have written this group of meditations to encourage you in your daily journey. They are meant to be read slowly and reflectively. At the end of each meditation are several scripture references for you to look up in your Bible and read.

Our spirits need to be fed and "medicated" by the word of God. He is the one who keeps us spiritually healthy; He is the Great Physician. I have found if I, for some reason, do not sit at the feet of Jesus, pouring out my love and listening for His guidance each morning, something is missing in my day.

Therefore, it is my prayer that as you sit in the presence of Jesus, you may feel His arms of love about you and be encouraged that He has been waiting for you with open arms. So, bow your head, close your eyes, and begin a conversation with Jesus, ask Him to fill you with His Holy Spirit who will give you wisdom and understanding.

"Rejoice in the Lord always; again I will say, rejoice... the peace of God, which surpasses all understanding, will guard your hearts and your minds in Christ Jesus."
Philippians 4:4, 7 NRSV

READ—PONDER—PRAY

Blessings,

Rev. Betty A Beach-Connell

DEDICATION

I dedicate this book of prayers, meditations, and scripture sentences to all the people who have encouraged me on my journey. They are my family, friends, pastors, the congregations whom I served, and strangers who unknowingly encouraged me by their questions. There are far too many to name...but, you know who you are.

I particularly would like to thank my husband, who has sacrificed much time reading my material and offering suggestions. I thank him, also, for making sure that I had nourishment in the form of food for my physical body, without which, I probably would have faded away. His encouragement is unmatched and goes far beyond, I'm sure, anything he could have foreseen. He is truly a partner in every sense of the word...for this I am very grateful. We walk together with the Lord.

Take Time

By
Rev. Betty A. Beach-Connell
5/28/85

Take time
Time to stand still and be
Be present in God's presence
Listening to his voice in creation.

Take Time
Time to become
Become all God has meant you to be
Accept yourself.

Take time
Time to be one of God's little children
Time to know you are held in the palm of His hand
Time to know that he is guiding you through-out the land
Take time—time to be His.

STAND BY ME

"My peace I give to you, not as the world gives..." John 14:27 MEV

The things of this world cannot give us lasting peace. When you give a child a new toy, they are thrilled to pieces, for a while. Then before long, you will see them casting the toy aside and playing with the box instead! Why is that? Because "things"—material things—have a limited shelf life. They are finite. Pretty soon, we are looking around for something else to give us pleasure.

I lift up a prayer for our children every day that goes something like this: Bless them, Lord, in doing and taking all the right steps to a better, more loving, and fulfilling life." It is a wonderful thing to see this prayer taking affect. Before we leave this earth, may we enjoy many years of enjoying the fruition of that prayer—that would indeed be a blessing.

"...but those that wait upon the Lord shall renew their strength; they shall mount up with wings as eagles." Isaiah 40:31 MEV

Psalm 89:15-17 Psalm 16:8 2Peter 1:2

ONE FOOT ON EARTH—ONE FOOT IN HEAVEN

"Let us hold tightly without wavering to the hope we affirm, for God can be trusted to keep His promise." Hebrews 10:23 NLT

There is no need to worry about tomorrow because (1) God has it all planned and under His control; (2) Tomorrow may never come. There is a song that states this great truth—it says: "Yesterday's gone, and tomorrow may never come, but we have this moment, today!" ("We Have This Moment, Today" by Bill & Gloria Gaither) This is why this moment is called the present—it is a gift from God—and that is where we must do our living.

"God is faithful, and by Him you were called to the fellowship of His Son, Jesus Christ our Lord." I Corinthians 1:9

Living today, with an eye toward the future, assures us that one day we will occupy a room in that mansion God has prepared for us in heaven. There is one caveat, however; I'm not talking about raucous living. What I am talking about is living a confident, committed, calm, and connected life as unto the Lord.

"This is the day the Lord has made, we will rejoice and be glad in it."
Psalm 118:24 MEV

How will you live it?

I John 1:3 Isaiah 49:7 Deuteronomy 7:9

COME TO ME AND LISTEN!!

"Come to me with your ears wide open. Listen, and you will find life. I will make an everlasting covenant with you. I will give you all the unfailing love I promised to David. Isaiah 55:3 NLT

When Daniel and his friends refused to bow down to other gods, even in the face of death, God protected them. Their enemies threw Meshach, Shadrach, and Abednego into the fiery furnace, but the fire did not consume them. In fact, those watching saw an extra person in the flames with them (Daniel 3:19-30)! This is proof that God is with us, even in the fieriest storms of life, **if** we follow His commands. He does not leave us nor forsake us (Hebrews 13:5). He protects us and will bring us up out of the mire and set our feet upon a rock—never to fall (Psalm 40:2). If we build our house upon that rock instead of in the sand, nothing—no storm—will ever be able to destroy it (Matthew 7:24-27).

You are the temple of the Lord. Fill your heart with God's love—the love you receive through reading His Word, prayer, and believing will give you strength and power to follow the path that God has prepared for you. Yogi Berra says, "When you come to a fork in the road, take it," (Berra-isms from the 50 greatest Yogi Berra quotes via the Internet) but I say, "Take the road that leads Home."

Which path will you take?

I Corinthians 3:16 I Corinthians 6:19 II Corinthians 6:16

REST IN ME, MY CHILD

"Remain in Me and I will remain in you." John 15:4a MEV

Lord, You are my shepherd. You supply everything I need. You lead me through the paths of life. You show me the way through the difficult times and lead me when I don't know the way; therefore, I shall not want (Psalm 23). Nothing can harm me while I am in Your presence. When I stand with You, even my enemies will tremble and not come near me.

Blessed are You, O Lord, my comforter, redeemer, and friend. Surely goodness and mercy shall follow me all the days of my life.

Psalm 23 Psalm 5:8 Psalm 19:7-9

THE SHEPHERD

*Surely goodness and mercy shall follow me
all the days of my life.
(Psalm 23:6) NRSV*

Lord, You are my shepherd; You lead me through the paths of life. You supply everything I need; therefore, I shall not want.

You guide me through the difficult times and lead me when I don't know the way.

Nothing can harm me while I am in Your presence.

When I stand with You, even my enemies will tremble and not come near me.

Blessed are You, O Lord, my comforter, redeemer, and friend.

Thinking about my family and looking at pictures of them fills me with great joy. Isn't it true we remember the good times we have had with loved ones rather than the bad times? Into each life, some rain must fall, otherwise how would we know that we were enjoying the sunlight? Each of our children have their own personalities. God created each one with characteristics that He knew would enhance them on their journey.

Miles separate us, but by the power of love, we are as close as a breath. The same is true of Jesus... He is as close to us as our skin. He breathes life into us by the power of His Holy Spirit. That is the same Spirit that binds families together, even though they are far apart.

Do not fret if you are far away from your loved ones—they are only a prayer away. God, through His Son, Jesus, and His Holy Spirit, can reach out to each one and draw you close as He envelopes all in His mighty, strong, loving arms. Embrace Him and you will be embracing those that you love.

John 6:56 I John 2:6 Galatians 2:20

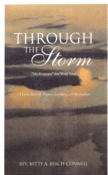

THROUGH THE STORM

"Medications for Your Soul"

This is a powerful collection of stories, prayers, and meditations focusing on the healing capabilities of God's Word, the Bible. To handle challenging times in life. As readers become aware of God's presence through every moment, the hope is they understand the need for God, Jesus, and the Holy Spirit. This book will touch lives and encourage the reader to have a closer walk with God through the reading of his Word, prayer, and meditation-all vital steps for peace and fulfillment.

Rev. Betty A. Beach-Connell

EMBRACING THE CALL

"God can lead you to places you never imagined"

An honest, heartfelt and exquisitely composed testimony of a real world facing real challenges to follow her calling. Too often we read about exotic people in exotic places, overcoming political oppression and militant violence just to be able to read a Bible; we thus forget that every call to ministry is just as special as any other, and the choice to obey is powerful and deeply affecting. The author's practical concerns - *What would we do for money? What would I do for my education? What would it be like to be a woman in the ministry? I had certainly never seen one!* - are relatable and highly engaging to readers. But she stepped out in faith: There were a lot of "ifs" and only one certainty. God had called me!

UNBURDENED

"Seek the Kingdom of God above all else, and live righteously, and he will give you everything you need."
Matthew 6:33 NLT

Thank you, Lord, for helping me from becoming unraveled. Thank you for offering us a way out of our Timeshare nightmare. We are, by the grace of God, to become ex-timeshare owners. We foolishly acquired three over the years. But today, we signed papers to transfer them to new owners. Yesterday is a day I do not want to repeat EVER AGAIN!

There came a moment when I heard clearly, in the midst of all the chaos, the voice of God telling me that we were on the right track and we should continue. It is hard to know the right path to take and who to listen to sometimes. It is then, especially, when we need to bow our heads and seek the Lord's guidance.

Help me, Lord, to ALWAYS hear Your still, small voice as I continue my journey. May I always keep You as my focal point and my main objective, no matter what anyone else may say.

It's wonderful to know that my life is hidden with Christ in God and also sealed by the Holy Spirit.

"Whatever your task, put yourselves into it, as done for the Lord and not for your masters," Colossians 3:23 NRSV

John 8:29 Colossians 3:23-24 Matthew 6:33

PLANS FOR GOOD

"I know the plans I have for you says the Lord, plans for peace and not for evil, to give you a future and a hope."
Jeremiah 29:11 MEV

When we walk close to Jesus, we feel safe—we are safe. We no longer walk in darkness, for He is the light of the world.

Sometimes the choices that we make are made outside the path that God has chosen for us. As a result, bad things happen that not only affect us, but many other people who love us. The effect is like a pebble thrown in the water—first there is a splash, out from which ripples stretch far and wide.

The good news is when we come back in stride with God, we find something amazing—He is there waiting and welcomes us with arms out-stretched saying, "Welcome home. I love you."

The Lord says,

"I will guide you along the best pathway for your life. I will advise you and watch over you. Do not be like a senseless horse or mule that needs a bit and bridle to keep it under control." Psalm 32:8-9 NLT

Psalm 32:7 Genesis 3:8-9 John 8:12

THIS IS THE MOMENT

*"The children of your people will live in security.
Their children's' children will thrive in Your Presence."*
Psalm 102:28 NLT

There is a swirl of unrest around me. Today we live in the shadow of terrorists hitting the World Trade Center in New York City (September 11, 2001), killing hundreds of innocent people, as well as at the Pentagon in Washington, DC. A plane full of people were killed after their plane was taken over by terrorists and crashed in a field in Shanksville, Pa. We shudder to think what will come next. **But**, no matter what—Jesus is by our side—all will be well in Him.

There is a swirl of unrest around me. Family members are suffering, and I feel helpless, but worry and fretting cannot help their cause. On the human level, there are many miles between us, and those miles separate us. But there is nothing that can separate us from the love of God; it is that love that holds us together even though we are apart.

Jesus died that we might live; He sent His Holy Spirit to convict, comfort, sustain, and give us power over all things— if we believe and call upon Him. God the Father, God the Son, God the Holy Spirit binds us together stronger than super glue. I must call upon Him and trust and believe. God is in charge. I must listen and follow His leading.

This is the moment in which all is well because God is with us, and He will make all things right. Now is the time to rejoice in the presence of God—no matter what. Indeed, if you put your burden before God, He will put in your hands everlasting peace.

Dear Lord, keep me, my family, and friends in the protection of your everlasting word—let Your blood cover all who believe in Your Name—the name above all names—Jesus.

When your knees feel shaky—kneel.
James 1:17 I Peter 1:22-23 James 4:8

DRAW NEAR TO ME

"I tell you the truth anyone who obeys my teaching will never die!" John 8:51 NLT

It took me many, many years to discover what I had been looking for—longing for. It is not that my parents and all my family didn't love me; they did and they showed it, but there was always something that seemed to be missing.

The one who I later learned was the "father of lies," the devil, had been offering me what I'll call, "good-looking" love. It looked good and felt good—for a while.

Then one day I found the missing link! I opened my mind and my heart—I began to hear the voice of God. He had broken through all the clutter, all the noise, all the lies that ole sloo-foot had been telling me and removed the veil so that I could see who really loved me. I could feel the love that I was looking for all those years. I was once again that little girl lying under the apple tree, looking up to the heavens asking, "Isn't there anyone to love me?" Only this time, I had found the answer—His name is Jesus.

What about you? Have you opened your heart and mind to Jesus? If you haven't, perhaps, now is the time.

Dear God, give me an inner strength that comes from you through Your Spirit. Christ be more and more in my life. In Your Holy Name, the name of Jesus, I pray. Amen

John 4:44 James 4:7-8

After the storm

——————————————

"The Lord is your guardian; the Lord is your shade at your right hand. The sun shall not harm you during the day, nor the moon during the night." Psalm 121:5-6 MEV

I AM WITH YOU

"For it was you who formed my inward parts; you knit me together in my mother's womb. Psalm 139:13 NRSV

Not one of your thoughts escapes my notice.

We are creations of God. He knows every part of us, even better than we know ourselves. He knows what we are thinking, so there is no need to try to act as though He doesn't. Sometimes we try to do and say things that do not reflect what we really think, just to try to fit in or to avoid confrontation. We can fool people, but never God.

Think of this—a person invents, puts together, every intricate part of a machine. That person knows exactly where each part is and how it works. That person even knows if any part of the machine is not working correctly. If it has a memory chip, that memory chip is like our brain—it tells the device what to do—just as our brain relates to us knowledge and through that knowledge directs our actions.

Our inventor is God. He created (made) us—He knows even the number of hairs on our heads; He knows every intricate part of our bodies. He even knows our thoughts because He is not only with us, He dwells within us. When we try to fool God, we are only fooling ourselves. So give thanks to God the Father, God the Son, and God the Holy Spirit—the one true God—who made you special and to live in the light of His love.

Thank you, God, for creating me—I am one of a kind. Thank You for making me special. You know me better than anyone else—You are my Lord and my Shepherd.

Psalm 139 Psalm 71:6 Jeremiah 1:5

IN HIS HANDS

"Be still and know that I am God." Psalm 46:10 NRSV

Begin each day with joyful expectation, watching to see what God will do. Let the dew of His presence refresh your mind and heart.

Dear Heavenly Father, help me to be still and put all my cares in Your hands and trust in You.

The scene of Jesus speaking as He sat in the house of Mary, Martha, and Lazarus in The Gospel of Luke, chapter 10:39-42, teaches us a very important lesson. Mary is chastised by her sister, Martha, for not helping her prepare the meal for their guest. Instead, she is sitting at the feet of Jesus, listening intently and lovingly to His words. Jesus responds to Martha saying that Mary has discovered what is really important and she should not be reprimanded for it.

Is Jesus saying that Mary should not help her sister? I don't think so. Is He saying that Martha should not busy herself with dinner preparations? I think not.

I think He is saying that Mary has discovered that before beginning her day, she should sit at the feet of Jesus and listen to His words which will guide her through the day.

<u>Before you rush into your day, take a few moments to pour out your love for Him by drinking in His words. Let His Holy Spirit fill you and ultimately guide and direct every decision you make.</u>

Only one thing is needful—that you sit at the feet of Jesus and pour out your love for Him.

Psalm 46:10 Luke 10:39-42 1 Corinthians 14:33 Joel 2:28

BEGIN EACH DAY

"For in him we live and move and exist." Acts 17:28 NLT

Begin each day in joyful expectation watching to see what God is going to do.

What a wonderful philosophy to live by! "He is all I need," we sing, and it is true. He IS all we need. We can look out at nature in awe; we see the birds, animals, trees, etc., but God is in so many other little things that happen around us every day. Are we so enamored by the vastness of God that we fail to see the minuscule things He does every day to make our lives livable?

I, for one, want to train myself to start looking for those so-called "little" things that God is doing all around me, and perhaps in me, every day. I know sometimes—probably most times—we see them in retrospect, but the important thing is we recognize God's hand at work in our everyday lives and give Him all the honor and glory.

God speaks to us:

"Grace and peace to you from the one who is, who always was, and who is still to come." Revelation 1:4b NLT

We speak to God:

"All glory to him who loves us and has freed us from our sins by shedding his blood for us." Revelation 1:5b NLT

Thank you, Lord Jesus, for your precious Holy Spirit sent to guide me daily. AMEN

2 Corinthians 12:9-10 Acts 17:28 Colossians 2:6-7 John 14:20

PLANNING—TRUSTING

"Trust in the Lord and He shall direct your path." Proverbs 3:5a; 6b MEV

Making lists of what I need to do for the day is something I enjoy. Then as I accomplish each task, I cross it off or put a check mark alongside it. I feel that the Lord is prompting me and calling me to do each and every thing on my list! I admit, sometimes my mind gets so full and rushed that I plow ahead of myself to accomplish everything I think I ought to do. But, and this is a big but, I always know and am aware of the Lord's presence and His guiding hand.

Please Lord, never let me wander from your presence and please, please, do not take your presence from me. Show me what you want me to do today. If you want me to make a list—so I will do. If you want me to sit and rest—please, give me a mind to do so. Help me, Lord, to say the right words to those that I love—and help me to show them that love. Help me to minister to members of our family in their times of trial; and I call upon You, O Lord, to surround them with Your Angels and fill their homes with Your Holy Spirit; wrap them in the blanket of Your love. Help me to remember that we can do the planning, but You direct our paths (Proverb 16:9).

When all is said and done:
This is the day the Lord has made, we will rejoice and be glad in it.
Psalms 118:24 MEV
AMEN

Come close to God and He will come close to you—Lord God, help us to know what we are to do.
James 4:13-15 Proverbs 3:5 Isaiah 40:28-31

PEACE

"In peace I will lie down and sleep, for you alone,
O Lord, will keep me safe."
Psalm 4:8 NLT

There are so many of us who have trouble sleeping. Likewise, there are many medications that claim they can give you a good night's sleep. There are numerous reasons why we cannot sleep, for instance: pain, worry over finances, what will the future hold for me if such-n-such, concern for our children and loved ones, abusive relationships—the list goes on and on.

But, will medication solve those problems? Will staying awake at night solve them? NO! The good news is this: Jesus holds the answer to the whole of life. He is our rock, our sustainer, and our peace.

The best medication is meditation. Jesus will help us lie down in peace, during which in the quietness of your spirit, He will speak to you and show you the way.

Thank you, God, for the promise of Your safety. Lord, give me perfect peace as I sleep tonight. In Jesus' name we pray. Amen

Psalm 4:6-8 Revelation 21:23

WHEN I WANDER

"Oh, Lord, I give my life to you. I trust in you, my God!"
Psalm 25:1-2 NLT

If you are like me, and I believe that many of you are, your mind tends to wander off course from time to time. You forget "Whose" you are and focus upon "who" you are. Your world may begin to fall in upon you and nothing seems possible. This is nothing more than taking your eyes off Jesus.

Remember when Peter was called to Jesus? The problem was that to get to Jesus, he had to walk on water. Could he do it? He could and he did—as long as he kept his eyes on Jesus. The minute he took his eyes off Jesus—and put his focus on his problem, walking on water—he began to sink (Matthew 14: 28-33). But Jesus reached out His hand and when Peter grabbed hold of it, he once again walked on the water. The same can be for us. As long as we keep our eyes on Jesus—keep our focus on Him and not on our problems—we too can "walk on water."

The good news is—Jesus (God) will never leave you nor forsake you (Hebrews 13:5). Just call out His name and He will come to you (Jeremiah 33:3).

Keep your eyes on Jesus
Look full in His wonderful face
He will fill you with His wonder and grace.

God lets you know, in so many ways, that whatever you go through, He will bring you out. He promises that the latter days will be better than the former. Thank you, Jesus. God will be there for you; He made a promise and He won't take it back.

Exodus 3:14 1 Corinthians 3:16 Psalm 25:14-15

REMEMBERED

"Search me, O God, and know my heart; test me and know my anxious thoughts. Point out anything in me that offends you, and lead me along the path of everlasting life. Psalm 139:23-24 NLT

Jesus is closer than the air we breathe.

Thanks be to God for creating me the way I am—a "masterpiece"—one of a kind. Thank you, God, for being with me when I wake up. Thank you, Father, for loving me and thank You for letting me know you. Thank You, Holy Spirit, for guiding me and directing me—even when I go kicking and screaming—through the journey You have chosen for me. I give God, Jesus, and the Holy Spirit all the honor and glory.

Be eager to know God's ways and follow His footsteps for God sent Christ, who never sinned, to be the offering for your sin, through whom you are made right with God.

Today is the first day of the rest of my life. Yesterday is gone and tomorrow may never be, so let me live today as I would want people to remember me. May I let Christ's light shine through me, so that others may see Him, because my life is not about me, it is about living in the sunshine of God's love that others might know Him. Let me be a blessing to someone today. Amen

Psalm 139:1-6 2 Corinthians 5:21

ENTRUST YOUR LOVED ONES TO ME

"...Abraham, Abraham!"
"Yes," Abraham replied, "Here I am!"
Genesis 22: 11 NLT

It was late in the afternoon. The phone rang and I recognized the voice of our son. He told me in calmness and strength that his sister, our youngest daughter, had an accident and she was in the hospital. The wind went out of me—I couldn't think, let alone speak! Our son went on to tell me what he knew about the accident. After the shock came the anger. The worse part—no, the worst part was my baby was hurt—but, this happened the night before and no one called us!!! Our baby girl was lying in a hospital, in ICU, and no one told us?

I wanted to get in a plane and fly to her side, but that wasn't possible. I was experiencing some ear problems and could not get on a plane, even though I wanted to. We were 1200 miles away, and it would take us 3 days to get to the hospital. I felt stuck. "Settle down," my husband told me. Thanks be to God, my faith kicked in. She was not alone... she had the support of her brother and sisters, her son, her fiancé, and her many friends and, most of all, I knew in my heart that God was watching over her.

The best thing that I could do was get down on my knees and pray. I also banded together all the prayer warriors I knew, and the prayers began to go out for our injured daughter. Please, dear Lord, heal her body, soul, and spirit. Continue to be with her and help her to feel your presence down this long road of recovery. Help us all hear You say, "Here I am." Amen

God give us an inner strength that comes from You, through Your Spirit. Christ be more and more in our lives—go with us and give us rest and peace.

Genesis 22:9-12 Ephesians 3:20 Exodus 33:14

A GOOD DAY

Today is a good day to be a good day
Because *"Today is the day the lord has made..."*
Ps. 118:24 MEV
Amen (Let it be)

Romans 8 tells us a great truth that we need to hear.

"So now there is no condemnation for those who belong to Christ Jesus. And because you belong to him, the power of the Holy Spirit has freed you from the power of sin that leads to death."(Vs 1-2 NLT)

Did you get the message? **You are free from sin when you belong to Jesus!** Do we ever sin again after we accept Jesus Christ into our hearts? Yes!! Human beings have finite minds and those finite minds have to make many choices—not always the right choices. Therefore, we fall into the trap of sin.

When you belong to Jesus, sin can still find a way into your life. Ole Sloo-Foot is always looking for a way to corrupt your life and lead you away from God. BUT—<u>and this is the key</u>—that sin, because of the love of Jesus and the power of the Holy Spirit living in you, that sin no longer has power over you. Ole Sloo-Foot cannot come near you.

When *you* sin, you go against the will of God. But rather, love God with all your heart, mind, strength, and soul, and love your neighbor as yourself. Then, when you do things outside that law, you have the opportunity to come to Jesus and ask for forgiveness. His death upon the cross assures us of that forgiveness. Jesus died taking the sins of the world upon Himself.

COME CLOSE TO GOD AND HE WILL COME CLOSE TO YOU.
God's love is the super glue that will never fail—
NO NEVER!
James 4:7 Romans 8:1-2 Isaiah 12:2,

WAIT WITH ME FOR A WHILE

"...you do not have because you do not ask." James 4:2 NRSV

Dear Lord, your touch is healing to me. Keep me in Your presence.

February, 2014 I published my first book, "Embracing the Call"—God can take you to places you never imagined. In the beginning, we did very well. Sales were happening over the Internet and the book-signings were going very well. I was receiving rave reviews, such as:
 The author's practical concerns—*What would we do for money? What would I do for my education? What would it be like to be a woman in the ministry? I had certainly never seen one!*—are relatable and highly engaging to readers. But she stepped out in faith: *There were a lot of "ifs" and only one certainty. God had called me.* Bravo, Pastor Betty.
 And this one: *"This book captures a woman's triumph through her ups and downs. It's such a motivating story about finding one's faith and living it. I recommend this book to anyone who ever faced a challenge or is looking to overcome something now. Thanks Rev. Betty for writing your truth!"*
 And this one—*I enjoyed reading your book! I couldn't lay it down as your life unfolded in the troubled times and balanced with the Lord's leading in your ministry!*
 I cried out—what's wrong, Lord? Why is everything coming to a standstill? I do not understand it—but, I know that You do, Lord. Please help me. I want You to be the center of my life, so please show me the way.
 The next day, the answer came. The Lord revealed to me through the meditation of the day what I needed to do. He said, "Wait with Me for a while. I have much to tell you. The

work I am doing in you is hidden at first. But eventually blossoms will burst forth, and abundant fruit will be born. Stay on the path with Me. Trust Me whole heartedly, letting My Spirit fill you with joy and peace."

I responded:
I TRUST YOU, LORD. DO WITH ME WHAT YOU WILL.
I Kings 8:23 Galatians 5:22-23 Matthew 7:7 2 Corinthians 12:7-9

THE OCEAN

"I pray that from his glorious, unlimited resources he will empower you with inner strength through his Spirit."
Ephesians 3:16 NLT

How vast, how deep, how wide, how powerful is the ocean. Standing on the shore, looking out at the sea, it seems that it goes on endlessly. Our Creator created a world in which His people could work, play, and experience the width, the length, the height, and the depth of His love. It is a masterpiece, put together with incomprehensible skill. And He made it accessible to us that we might build our relationship with Him and each other.

God's love is as vast as the ocean and beyond—it is immeasurable.

The next time you see the ocean, let it remind you of the love God has for you. His love has no boundaries or obstacles—it is all-powerful and beats all odds. This is what humanity is searching for, and it is right there for everyone to receive. All we have to do is say, *"Come in, Lord Jesus."* And then He says, *"Here I am, follow Me."*

May we believe that Jesus the Son of God was sent here by God the Father, and that Jesus willingly came and died for the whole world, so that each one of us could have a chance to accept and believe in Him and be forgiven and receive eternal life with Him.

Revelation 22:17 John 6:37 Ephesians 3:16-19

And so I tell you, keep on asking and you will receive what you ask for. Keep on seeking and you will find. Keep on knocking, and the door will be opened to you. For everyone who asks, receives. Everyone who seeks, finds. And to everyone who knocks, the door will be opened.

Luke 11:9-10 MEV

CONFIDENCE

"Commit your actions to the Lord and your plans will succeed." ... "We can make our plans, but the Lord determines our steps." Proverbs 16:3, 9 NLT

Making plans, being prepared, is a good thing, but then there is the execution of those plans. I read the chapters, made my notes, and wondered how the class would go. What if someone asked a question that I didn't have an answer for? What if someone didn't agree with me? How would I handle it? What if... what if... what if?

Then God spoke to me through His word..."*Commit everything you do to the Lord. Trust Him, and He will help you*" *(Psalm 37:5).* He spoke to me through the meditations of the morning (just in case I didn't get it the first time). "Trust Me enough to let things happen without striving to predict or control them" (Jesus Calling by Sarah Young, page 297). I could feel myself relax and my striving turned to joy and excitement, wondering what I was going to do.

There is nothing we can do under our own strength, intelligence, or personality without the help of the Lord. I got off my high horse and allowed God to chauffer me through the task He had given me.

God speaks to you:
*"And this same God who takes care of me will supply all your needs from His glorious riches, which have been given to us in Christ Jesus." (Philippians 4:19)*NLT

Proverbs 8:20-21 I Peter 2:23-25 Isaiah 53:6

GOD SPEAKS

"Listen, and I will tell you a great mystery..."
I Corinthians 15:51 NRSV

I lie in bed looking out my window at the reflection in the lanai window of the sun rising. Every morning, I awake with the bright sunlight shining in my eyes; however, this morning, this wasn't the case. As I continued to watch the reflection, I noticed some very black clouds that shielded the sun, then suddenly the sun emerged from behind them! This routine continued for quite some time. The black clouds were trying their darndest to block out the light.
Then I had a thought! "This is what happens in life!" There are times when all seems dark and lost; there are times when all is right and sunny. Troubles come and troubles go, but the light is always there—somewhere—it will appear just at the right time and brighten your day.
God speaks in the midst of darkness, telling us that

"Joy will come in the morning," (Psalm 30:5)
"Do not be afraid," (Joshua 1:9)
"I will never leave you nor forsake you..." (Hebrews 13:5).

As sure as the sun is shining behind those black clouds, God's presence is with you—always.
God will equip you with the necessary resources you need to do any work He has for you. So, do not be anxious in anything (Philippians 4:6) and know that He knows what lies ahead of you; He will go before you.

"May the Lord smile on you and be gracious to you. May the Lord show you His favor and give you His peace." (Numbers 6:25-26)

I Thessalonians 4:13-18 Philippians 3:21 Psalm 17:15

EYES THAT SEE

"You must not make for yourself an idol of any kind or an image of anything in the heavens or on the earth or on the sea. ...I, the Lord, your God...will not tolerate your affections for any other gods... you must not bow down to them or worship them..."
Exodus 20:4-5 NLT

Beware of seeing yourself through someone else's eyes. How is it possible that you could know what they really think of you? Don't try to please everyone; it is impossible, you will only end up offending someone and making yourself miserable. Pleasing others so that they will think well of you borders on idolatry.

Our Lord commands us not to make for ourselves idols. He says,

"[I] will not tolerate your affection for any other gods"
(Exodus 20:5).

Take your eyes off yourself and put them on Jesus who loves you, even with all your warts. He, and He alone, can and will make something beautiful out of you and your life. You will be a testament to others of the beauty that God creates.

Lord, continue to increase my faith so that I may receive Your promises and live an abundant life, in which I will be able to serve You. Amen

Joshua 24:15 Exodus 23:25 Matthew 4:10

MY PRAYER

*"Devote yourselves to prayer with an alert
mind and a thankful heart."*
Colossians 4:2 NLT

Thank you, Lord, for always being as near as a heartbeat. All the way you will lead me, all I have to do is follow. You are truly the way, the truth, and the life, not just for me, but for all who will call upon Your name.

Two of our girls were coming for a visit. We were very excited that we were going to be able to spend some time with them. We would be able to catch up on the lapsed time and just be together. Then the news was given to us—quite innocently—that one of them would only be with us for a night—and they would both be going to the seashore for a couple of days. Somehow our concept of visiting and theirs didn't quite mesh.

I'm happy for them, of course, but when would we have time to be together? I was hoping for some mother and daughter time—you know, just sitting, talking, looking at pictures, doing nothing special—just being together. I have to give it all to You, Lord. If it be Your Will, it will be.

More than anything, Lord, please help all of us to keep an open mind and not say anything that could be taken as controlling or directive. After all, these "girls" are women now and are living their own lives.

Dear Lord, please guide and direct all of our children and grandchildren. Thank you, Father, for letting me vent—thank You for listening. Open my ears that I may hear, my eyes that I may see, and my mouth that I may speak in love.

John 14:6 Colossians 4:2

His Grace

"Be careful how you live." Ephesians 5:15 NLT

Lord, help me to hide Your word in my heart that I may not sin against you. Your word is my strength and my shield. Thank you, Lord.
 Blessed be this day that I may live it for You, O Lord. Instill within me an attitude of peace, relaxing my desires to conform to yours.

*"This is the day the Lord has made.
We will rejoice and be glad in it"*
(Psalm 118:24)NLT

 We have spent a wonderful time with two of our girls. We have reminisced, laughed, and (almost) cried together. Now the sisters are off to the beach to spend a few hours with each other. It is beautiful to see relationships renewed—help them to renew their relationship with You, O Lord. May they see You in the ocean, stars, the sky, and in all creation. May they feel Your power as You wrap Your arms of love around them. Thank You, O Lord, for the blessings of our children.

"Make the most of every opportunity in these evil days."
Ephesians 5:16 NLT

 You know it is only by the grace of God that we are able to do all these things... not in my strength, Lord, but by Your Grace...

Ephesians 5:15-1 Psalm 119:105

HELP ME, HOLY SPIRIT

"Understand this my brothers and sisters: You must all be quick to listen, slow to speak, and slow to get angry."
James 1:19 NLT

Forgive me, Lord, for any misdeeds I may have committed today; bless me for all the things I did right. I come to You tonight as one who feels blessed...

- blessed to be called Your child;
- blessed by the one You gave me to be my husband;
- blessed for the children You allowed me to call my own—when I know they really belong to You;
- blessed to be safe in a world of turmoil.

Teach me, Lord, to be a good wife.
Teach me to think before I speak.
Teach me to do Your will, which is contained in Your Word.
Teach me to read Your Word that I may know Your will for my life.

This was the day that You made, and I have found joy in it. Thank You, Jesus.

Father, thank you for another day. Teach me to be a doer of Your word and not a hearer only. Thank you, Father, for drawing me to your word and never giving up on me.

Proverbs 12:18 James 1:19 Ephesians 4:29

EVEN BEFORE I KNEW YOU

"Holy, holy, holy is the Lord of Heaven's Armies! The whole earth is full of His glory!" Isaiah 6:3 NLT

Dear Lord, yesterday we were graced with your clouds. It was a blessing to have a cloudy day. Strange, isn't it? To be happy because the sun isn't shining. But, you see, that meant we didn't have to feel guilty for sitting around doing nothing. I was feeling very fatigued, I could barely pick my arms up to hold the newspaper, and we both didn't feel well: Your clouds allowed us to rest.

Today, though, You graced us with Your beautiful sunshine. Having been refreshed, we were able to enjoy its light and warmth. It took such a miracle to hang the clouds in space and place the sun where it can give us life instead of death. There is no other who could have created those miracles.

Thank you, Lord, for the ability to be aware of Your presence in the miracles of nature. Even before I knew You, I was blessed by the trees, flowers, sun, rain, birds, animals, etc.; even though I had no knowledge of Your existence, You blessed me with Your creation. How deprived I was not to know—or if I knew, not to acknowledge—Your Presence. But, Praise God, once I was blind and now I see—may I never be blind again.

The Lord gives us strength to do things that we never imagined we could do. He gives us strength to face and endure when we may have wanted to quit.

Father God, bless Your Holy Name. Father, please help me to hear You, to understand You, and to obey You. May my heart always be open to You and You alone. In Jesus' Name. Amen

Psalm 27:2 Isaiah 6:3

VALLEY OF THE SHEPHERD

*"He lets me rest in green meadows;
he leads me beside peaceful streams."
Psalm 23:2 NLT*

Once upon a time, there was a little girl named Betsy. Betsy would love to be out in the orchard, or woods, or romping through the fields of her fathers' farm. She loved the birds and flowers and the animals. She loved the wild berries that she picked which grew along the fences and stone walls. Betsy was at peace as she played alone among the natural things of life. She felt loved. She was in the valley of the Shepherd.

How can that sense of peace be recaptured in the fast world we live in today? Do children ever breathe in fresh clean air and commune with nature? I'm afraid we are moving too fast and missing too much—one day we may even fly off this planet into the abyss!

God calls us to stop, look, and listen. Stop and take a few breaths; look around at what He has created for our peaceful pleasure; and listen to His still, small voice as heard through the sounds of nature that sing its sweet melody to us. If we do, our spirits will become quiet, allowing His love to shine through us to others—making this a better world, the valley of the Shepherd.

"He renews my strength. He guides me along right paths, bringing honor to His name." Psalm 23:3 NLT
Psalm 23:2-3 Genesis 2:2-3 Luke 1:78-79

THE LOOKING GLASS

"My presence will go with you, and I will give you rest."
Exodus 33:14 NRSV

Jesus has invested His life in me. How would I feel if something in which I had invested everything suddenly turned against me or refused to do that which it was created to do? Abandoned... betrayed. Likewise, when I turn myself away from Jesus, it crushes Him... but still, He never stops loving me.

A parent gives all they have to make it possible for their child to have a good life, perhaps a better life than they had, and suddenly that child turns against the parent for a myriad of reasons. Whatever the cause, the parent feels a sense of remorse and a longing for the child and what could've been— their efforts had gone unrealized. Jesus gave even more for us—He gave His life, His all.

Help me, Lord, to take my eyes off of myself and put them on the one who loves me more than life itself. When I look in the mirror, help me to see someone who reflects the love of Christ, regardless of the image I see in the glass. No greater sacrifice was made by no man than the one God made for each one of us—He gave His only Son that we might not perish, but shall have eternal life (John 3:16). Let me not let that sacrifice be made in vain.

"For God so loved the world that he gave his only Son, so that everyone who believes in him may not perish but may have eternal life." John 3:16 NRSV

Isaiah 63:9 Acts 9:4 Matthew 25:40

JUMP!!

"In the beginning God created the heavens and the earth... Then God saw that it was good." Genesis 1:1ff NLT

Blessed be the Lord God who made heaven and earth and all its inhabitants.

I heard a story about a house that was on fire. Inside the house was a little boy who stood by the window calling for help. His father stood below and was calling out to him to jump. The little boy was scared and didn't want to jump.

The little boy yelled, "I can't; I can't see you!"

The father called back, "That doesn't matter, son, I can see you. Jump!"

Many times, you may be afraid to jump, also. You hear God calling you forward but are afraid because you cannot see the future. God calls out to you —"That doesn't matter, my child, I can see you. Jump, I'm here for you."

When you do jump, even though you do not understand or cannot imagine why, you are walking by faith, not by sight (Zechariah 4:6). When God calls you to walk through a door, He promises to never leave you nor forsake you (Hebrews 13:5). He will provide all your needs (Philippians 4:19).

Go for it! "Jump," his father said, "I will catch you!"

Dear Lord, show me the way that You want me to go. Sometimes I have a very hard and thick head. Am I doing what You want me to do? I know you know what is ahead, Lord—help me to have faith; help me to be patient; help me not to lose confidence. In Jesus' name I pray. Amen

Proverbs 8:20-21 Joshua 1:5 Romans 8:35-39

LISTEN TO HIS VOICE

"Do not let your hearts be troubled, and do not let them be afraid. The peace I give is sufficient for you." John 14:27 NRSV

"Trust Me in the midst of a messy day. Seek My face, and I will share My mind with you, opening your eyes to See things from My perspective." There are no circumstances that can touch the peace that God gives me—and you.

Here on earth you will have many sorrows, but though you may have sorrow now, in time you will rejoice, and no one can take away your joy. God, Himself, has given us His SON and the Son has left us His Holy Spirit who comforts us in every way. He offers Himself to lead us and guide us along our journey—in every situation and circumstance He says, "Call upon Me and I will answer" (Jeremiah 33:3).

Lord, guide me along Your path today. May I be a blessing to someone today. Strengthen me, O Lord, to do Thy Will. In Jesus' name...

John 16:33 Psalm 105:4

CALLED

By
Rev. Betty A. Beach-Connell
6/7/85

God you have created me
I am who I am.

You have called me
And you have chosen me.

First fruits I give you
All that I am is yours.

There is nothing that comes before you
Not money, not position—nothing.

The old has passed away
The new has been formed.

Glory be to God
Alleluia, Alleluia!

STAY FOCUSED

"Trust in the Lord with all your heart and lean not on your own understanding." Proverbs 3:5 MEV

Jesus offers rest for your soul as well as refreshment for your mind and body—focus on Him not on whatever problem or circumstance you are facing. When we wander away from the Lord, our thoughts become empty; fear and frustration creep in.

*"Delight yourself in the Lord and
he will give you the desires of your heart."
Psalm 37:4 MEV*

As believers, we need to be in continual prayer for God to soften hearts and fill us with His wisdom. Pray for our Pastors to preach the Word of God; that teachers will exhibit manners, compassion, and kindness to their students; and that the leaders of the nations will find peaceful solutions to the problems that plague us. Pray that the hungry will be fed; the homeless will find shelter; and that relationships will be mended. We pray with thankfulness for God is always listening.
And finally,

"Be still in the presence of the Lord, and wait patiently for him to act. Don't worry about evil people who prosper or fret about their wicked schemes. Stop being angry! Turn from your rage! Do not lose your temper—it only leads to harm. For the wicked will be destroyed, but those who trust in the Lord will possess the land." Psalm 37:7-9 NLT

Dear, Lord Jesus, give me your wisdom and understanding. Teach me Your ways that I may live the abundant life that you have for me. Help me to forgive as You have forgiven me. Bless me this day. In Jesus' name...AMEN

Psalm 131:2 Psalm 21:6 Psalm 37:24

THE THIEF AND THE SHEPHERD

"The thief's purpose is to steal and kill and destroy. My purpose is to give them a rich and satisfying life."
John 10:10 NLT

Give this some good, honest thought. A thief comes in and takes what is not his own. A shepherd takes care of the flock with love and compassion and acceptance. The thief uses the darkness to cover his presence as he lurks about. The shepherd's light shines through even in the darkness and lights our path. The shepherd's light dispels the thief's darkness; it separates the evil from the good. Therefore, evil cannot have control over your life when the Shepherd (Jesus Christ) is present in it.

To enter the sheepfold, we must come in through the gate—any other way is the way of the thief. In other words, the only way is to ask Jesus into your heart by asking Him to forgive you of your sin (anything done in disobedience of God's will), humbling yourself before your God. Trust and believe that God is always working for your good. Relinquish control of your life—you cannot do it on your own—God knows you better than you know yourself.

"...and you shall call His name Jesus, for He shall save His people from their sins." Matthew 1:21 MEV

That includes you and me, if we will give our lives to Him.

Matthew 1:23 John 10:10-11 I Peter 2:23-25

STRENGTH IN WEAKNESS

"And the Holy Spirit helps us in our weakness."
Romans 8:26 NLT

A task lay before me—I didn't know how I was going to be able to do it. All I could think of is, "I've never done this before!" At the moment, I didn't even know how to start! I thought of the preparations. I thought of the people who would be present. Would they like me? Would they agree with what I was saying? Would they even understand? The butterflies in my stomach were flapping their wings so hard, I could hardly breathe! My quest to be in control of everything was suffocating me! For a time I had forgotten...

I had forgotten that only in Christ can all things be accomplished. I had forgotten whose I was and who was ultimately in control. I had forgotten that God had created me—He knew me so well, even the number of hairs upon my head—and He gave me Jesus as my example of love—and Jesus's death and resurrection gave me the power of the Holy Spirit to guide me. There wasn't really anything to worry about—I had God's army on my side!

He has you in the palm of His hand, and He will not let you fall. He sends His angels to have charge over you so that you will not stumble, but if you do, He promises to pick you up (Matthew 4:6; Psalm 91:1). What an awesome God we serve!

God's love is the super glue that will never fail. Thank you, God, for loving me so much, even when I do not do or think as I should. Please keep praying for me. (John 17)

Isaiah 42:3 Isaiah 54:10 Romans 8:26

HUFF AND PUFF

"Anyone who listens to my teaching and follows it is wise, like a person who builds a house on solid rock."
Matthew 7:24NLT

Once upon a time, there were three little pigs. Each one built a house. One was built with sand; one was built with straw; and one was built with brick. I know you probably know the nursery rhyme, but bear with me; I do have a point to all of this. Which one do you suppose withstood the wind and the rains? The one built with sand, the one built with straw, the one built with brick?

Well, as you know, the big, bad wolf came and tried to blow the houses down. The one made with sand blew away easily, as did the one built with straw. These two little pigs did not plan well—they didn't read the manual. The third little piggy's house withstood the raging of the big, bad wolf who went away never to bother that little piggy again.

Now put the big, bad wolf in the place of Satan who lurks around looking for ways to destroy you. He pretends to be your friend, when all the while, he wants to steal all of your joy. On the other hand, the pig whose house withstood the storm represents those who put their trust in Jesus. They have read the manual—the Holy Bible, God's story of love and redemption—just as the little pig read his manual before he built his house of bricks.

It is important to trust the Lord, even when things don't seem to make any sense at all. No matter how much the enemy comes against you, you will praise your God, for He has already won the victory.

May you worship the God of heaven and earth; may He help you to never turn away from Him, that you may enter into His place of sweet peace.

Psalm 42:7 Psalm 95:1-2 Matthew 7:24-25

HE IS LORD

"I am convinced that nothing can ever separate us from God's love. Neither death nor life, neither angels nor demons, neither our fears for today nor our worries about tomorrow—not even the powers of hell can separate us from God's love. No power in the sky above or in the earth below—indeed, nothing in all creation will ever be able to separate us from the love of God that is revealed in Christ Jesus our Lord." Romans 8:38-39NLT

Nothing can separate me from your love, Jesus.

Help me, Lord, to remember to repeat these words as I go through my day. Each and every day remind me, Lord, that nothing can happen to me as long as I depend upon You. Nothing in all creation can overtake me, because You have my name engraved upon Your hands and hold me securely in Your presence. My responsibility is to trust and be faithful.

"Delight yourself in the Lord and
He will give you the desires of your heart."
Psalm 37:4 NRSV

Romans 8:38-39 Joshua 1:5 Isaiah 49:15-16

WHAT IS NORMAL?

*"Suddenly, Jesus was standing there among them!
'Peace be with you,' he said."*
John 20:19 NLT

Slow down and quiet your mind so that you will be able to hear Jesus bestowing upon you His resurrection blessing—"Peace be with you."

"Lord, you are teaching me that I am still in ministry for you, I don't need to be out running myself ragged. But I suspect it will be a long time before I will be fully rested up." This may be your lament, as well.

You may wish that you could get back to your "normal" life as I do—but this may be the new normal. Life changes as we grow older. It takes some unprecedented twists and turns. This may be the path that God had planned for you. You see, wherever we are, God is there, also—that is the important thing.

Whatever you used to do in ministry for the Lord, you can still do, but in a different way. Perhaps, you used to drive from place to place, visiting people. Now you can still do that, only by phone or sending a card; maybe you worked at the church in one of its ministries, but cannot any longer—you can still be an encouragement for others and someone who can answer questions about the thrift shop or the dinner, etc.

Dear Lord, help me to remember that wherever I am, You are also, and I can dispense of Your love with my words and actions. Bless me this day, O Lord, as I look for your guidance and direction. Show me the way you want me to go. I pray that I will hear You saying, "Peace be still."

Colossians 1:27 Matthew 28:20 John 20:19

MY VOICE IN THE MORNING

*"The human mind plans the way,
but the Lord directs the steps."*
Proverbs 16:9 NRSV

Thank you, Lord, for this new day. I am anxious to find out what You have planned for me. I know what I think I have planned, but You, Lord, direct my path. Take me, Lord, where you want me to go.

Yesterday we planned our steps, or so we thought—we went to the thrift shop to deliver some more "stuff," then to the bank to make a deposit; we shopped for groceries; and went to the drug store to pick up a prescription. Each place, as we discovered, was directed by You, Lord.

There were ladies who needed a listening ear—a husband who was going for tests of his sinuses, they were newly married; another who has had surgery on her arm and needs to understand that she needs to be careful; ladies who were concerned about me and the results of my CT scan; a lady in the grocery store who we noticed was shopping strangely—picking up, squeezing, re-arranging, and then not buying—putting it back; she turned up right behind us at the check-out—distressing at first, but then she looked at me and smiled and told me something we had in our cart was the first thing the doctor took away from her husband. I asked, "Why?" And that was enough to open the flood gates. She told me her story how they traveled together and enjoyed one another's company, but now that was no more because of his deteriorating health. She started to cry. I put my hands on her shoulder and said I was so sorry and that God would help her through. She looked at me with hope in her eyes and said, "That's the only way I've been making it!"

Only God can quench your thirst. Only He is greater than water.

O, Lord, with joy unspeakable and full of glory.

Weeping may endure at night, but joy comes in the morning.

If you put your burden before God, He will put in your hands everlasting peace.

Psalm 5:3 Psalm 63:1 Philippians 4:13

A LETTER TO JESUS

Dear Jesus,
    I know you are OK, but I just have to ask—"How are you?" I sure do give you a hard time. I don't know why you put up with me. I know it seems like I am ignoring you because I haven't written in a few days, but I am sincere when I say, I know you are right here with me every moment.
    It is just that I am allowing "busy" to take up all my time of late. I need your help in kicking "busy" in the pants, so that I can get back to what I think I am called to do—write to tell others of your marvelous grace and love for them.
    I know that you cannot come back until everyone has at least had the opportunity to hear about you. After they have heard, it is their responsibility to make their choice whether to accept your love or not.
    You have said that our trials and tribulations—our sufferings—are not just to get our attention, but to share with others so they will know the right path to take. So, Jesus, help me to tell "busy" to go take a flying leap for himself!

Love,
Your Child,

2 Corinthians 1:3-4

"Look at the birds of the air, for they do not sow, nor do they reap, nor gather in barns. Yet your heavenly Father feeds them. Are you not much better than they?
Matthew 6:26 MEV

LEAVE IT TO GOD

"Wait on the Lord; be strong..." Psalm 27:14 NRSV

We took a bus trip; we didn't know our destination, although, we knew what was waiting for us at the end of the trip. We knew it would take us two hours to arrive at the river and board the paddlewheel boat that would take us on a short cruise up the river—what we didn't know was where it was located! In short, we trusted the leaders of the trip and, especially, our bus driver to take us where we needed to go.

As we journey through life, we "sometimes" know our goal but not the route to get there. We make our short-range and our long-range plans—sometimes they work and sometimes they do not. When our plans come from our head, it is "our" plan, but when they come from our heart, it is God's plan and that's the difference between the "sometimes."

Proverbs 16:9 says,

"A man's heart devises his way, but the Lord directs his steps."

And Psalm 37:4 says,

"Delight yourself in the Lord, and He will give you the desires of your heart."

Look to God as your bus driver who knows the way. He will take you to the place of peace and success. God will take care of you (Jeremiah 29:11-12).

Psalm 27:13-14 Exodus 15:13

A BOUQUET

"Give thanks always for all things to God the Father in the name of our Lord Jesus Christ...Ephesians 5:20 MEV

I always loved to walk in the woods. When I was young, I used to pick a bouquet of wild flowers to give to my mom whom I could usually find in our kitchen baking bread or pies or cooking our next meal. By the time I returned from my romp in the woods, the flowers were mostly wilted, but Mom received them as though they were a bouquet of fresh roses.

Our sorrows, misgivings, and stressful situations represent those wilted flowers that I offered to my mom. Sometimes we can carry them hidden inside of us for too long. But, when we address the issue and give thanks for each one, it is like putting those flowers in water—it gives us new life.

Offer God your wilted flowers, your hurts and sorrows; thank Him even in the midst of your darkest moments, not because you are suffering, but because God never leaves you in your suffering. Giving thanks to God opens the flood gates of living water and fills your heart with gratitude; you hold in your hands a bouquet—not wilted dreams and hopes, but a beautiful bouquet—representing love, peace, joy, patience, gentleness, goodness, faith, meekness, and self-control (Galatians 5:22-23).

Give thanks with a grateful heart.

Romans 8:38-39 Psalm 4:7-8 Psalm 18:1 Psalm 89:15-18

PERCEPTION

"For now we see as through a glass, dimly, but then, face to face. Now I know in part, but then I shall know, even as I also am known." I Corinthians 13:12 MEV

How we perceive ourselves (and others) gives us opportunity for growth and depth. As we look into a mirror, the reflection shows us what other people see—or does it? The truth is, mostly, we see only what we want to see—depending upon our own state of being. However, the true reflection helps us to see even our flaws; it encourages us to move forward and become the image that we were intended to be.

Wanting others to see us as we think we should be seen doesn't always, nor does it completely, depend upon us. It depends, more fully, upon others with whom you come in contact. It is their responsibility to accept and, perhaps, make an attitude adjustment. For it is true, "we see through the mirror dimly," until we see Jesus.

When others take you wrongly, first check yourself; second, examine the situation; then, last but not least, try to understand the situation of the other person. Never take it personally!

And most importantly, Christ Jesus calls you to *"love one another, as He has loved you," (John 15:9, 17)...* even your enemies *(Matthew 5:44).*

II Corinthians 5:7 I John 3:2 John 15:9-10 Matthew 5:44

EMANUEL

(God with Us)
*"You are my refuge and my shield;
Your word is the source of hope."*
Psalm 119:114 NLT

"Emanuel, Emanuel," we sing as though to begin a love letter to God, the letter that tells Him that we are aware of His Presence and want to share in His glory. Our hearts are overflowing in fellowship with God and one another. We are high on love!

Then we leave the confines and safety of the sanctuary, and the world smacks us square in the face! What happened? Nothing is different! I still have to figure out how to pay my bills; I still feel hurt over something someone said or did; I still have all my work laid out before me. Nothing on the outside has changed—but, it feels different.

What God wants you to know is He is with you—more than that—He goes before you. Spending a few moments each day with Him will guide and direct you in the way you should go. Your journey (life) without recognizing God's love through His Son, Jesus, is merely a series of guesses at every turn. But God says, "I am with you; call upon Me and I will direct your path." There will be a few stumbles, but He promises to catch you.

Thank you, Lord for loving me.

Ephesians 3:20 Hebrews 13:8 Ecclesiastes 1:2 Proverbs 3:6

WHAT CAN I GIVE?

*"And now faith, hope, and love abide these three;
and the greatest of these is love."
I Corinthians 13:13 NRSV*

One of my favorite Christmas songs is "The Little Drummer Boy." It tells a story of many bringing beautiful gifts—gifts of great splendor—to the Christ Child who was born in the manger. But there was one small boy who was very poor—all he was able to do was play a tune on his drum for the Baby Jesus.

The little boy began to play, "Pa rum pa rum pum, pa rum pa rum pum." He played with all the love his little heart held. The song tells us that when the Baby Jesus heard the little drummer boy's song, He smiled. The gift of his love was all the Baby Jesus needed or wanted.

We struggle and strive for the perfect gift. We spend far more than we can afford and struggle to pay off our credit cards for the rest of the year. Then next Christmas we start all over again. The story of the Little Drummer Boy tells us a different story and shows us a different way. There are gifts that keep on giving, rather than taking, such as: the gift of faith, the best present you can give a child; the gift of hope, Christmas reminds us that the darkness cannot overcome the light; the gift of love, sometimes all we want is for someone to hold us.

Faith, hope, and love are not only the best Christmas gifts, they are the best things in life! And they keep on giving!

*Luke 2:10-12 Matthew 1:23 Matthew 2:11b
Matthew 2:10-11a*

MORE THAN A DAY

When they saw the star they rejoiced with great excitement; and when they came into the house they saw the young child with Mary His mother; and they fell down and worshipped him." Matthew 2:10-11a MEV

A day which we call Christmas comes around once a year—we have designated that day to be December 25th. We make many preparations to celebrate this Blessed Day. We shop, clean, cook, send cards, decorate, and write our Christmas letters—some describing what our year has been like and some focusing on the meaning of Christmas. The stores are excited because it is a time of great economic gain. People are hurrying and scurrying about. Choirs are preparing their cantatas and pastors their Christmas Eve services. And, oh yes, there are the parties!

This year, amidst all of this, God invites you to stop for a moment and look into the manger—at the Baby Jesus and the love that surrounds Him. Allow yourself to be pulled into the scene. Breathe in the fragrance of the stable and enter into the peace and love that it offers.

As you experience His Presence, Christmas will live all year in your heart. It will become more than giving and receiving presents on this one day—for His Presence is a gift that keeps on giving.

Luke 2:10 John 3:16 Matthew 1:20-21 John 3:17

WHO AM I?

"...what are human beings that you are mindful of them?"
Hebrews 2:6 NRSV

It has been a mystery—a question that has been asked since the beginning of time—"Who am I, Lord, that you have loved me and protected me?" God has created us in His image and made us a little lower than the angels and gave us dominion (put us in charge; to care for) over all creation. Why?

I believe the answer is because we are family. This is a concept that has lost a little of its glimmer. There are so many families that are shattered. They are not only separated by miles, but, even worse, by tragedy and words. Our familial relationship with God is no different—we separate ourselves from Him in similar ways. We do not acknowledge His Presence and, therefore, cannot receive the gifts He has for us.

Stop and think, how have you gotten as far as you have? Your own skill? Your own thinking? Your own hard work? YES! YES! YES! But there is more. Think about this—without God's protection, you may have died in that accident; the credit card company may have sued you and you would've lost your life savings; or your son or daughter may have never come home again.

Think about your life; thank God in all things. Do not ever forget He is the most important member of your family.

I Chronicles 17:16 Psalm 144:3-4 Hebrews 2:6ff

A VISION

"Bless the Lord, O my soul." Psalm 104:1 NRSV

There are times when I wish I was able to paint a picture of what I am seeing in my mind—and this is one of those times. In reading Psalm 104, I have been given a glorious picture of God!! Perhaps it is too glorious to be captured on canvas by anyone but Michelangelo. Try and picture it:

God is clothed in light as we would wrap a blanket around ourselves; He is wrapped in light. All I can see is a big swirl of light. The light stretches itself out, as one would in putting up a tent, and the heavens are filled with His Presence.

The waters become the foundation for God's throne room. It is the place in which He sits wrapped in light and looks out over His Kingdom. The winds move through the great expanse and on them are the clouds which are His chariots. The winds become His messengers and the fire and flames His ministers. Such a vision of power wrapped in love!

We are wrapped in the glory of the Lord—those who believe and trust in the Word, for "the Word was God" (John 1:1). Those who follow Him have all that He is, was, and will ever be (Revelation 1:8) as their source of strength and power. We are called to go forth into all the world and make disciples in the name of Jesus Christ (Matthew 28:19).

Psalm 104:1-5 Amos 9:5a-6 Isaiah 19:1 Hebrews 1:7

FOLLOW THE STAR

*"And the star which they saw in the
East went before them..."*
Matthew 2:9 MEV

The Wise Men heard of the birth of the one called "The Christ Child" and wanted to see him. They were from afar, probably Persia. Their visit was all in God's plan, for a star appeared in the East. That was meaningful to the Wise Men because they were astronomers and accustomed to studying the stars. They followed the star as it led them to the manger where the Christ Child lay. There they fell down and worshipped Him and presented Him with gifts.

We, too, have a star to follow. God has a plan for each of us, also. The question is will we follow?

The story of the "Three Kings" is a story which is meant to teach us that if we follow the light, it will lead us to Jesus. There we will be filled with awe and overcome with joy as we stand in His presence.

Christmas is a time to remember our commitment to the Christ Child who was born to show us how to love God and one another. We give each other gifts, sharing our love—the love shown to each of us—unconditionally.

This Christmas, if you haven't followed the star leading to Jesus, I pray you consider doing so. Ask Him for forgiveness and open your heart to Him—He is waiting just for you. He is the greatest gift you will ever receive!

Luke 1:35 John 1:14 Matthew 2:9-11 Luke 1: 78-79

PEACE

"Let not your heart be troubled neither let it be afraid."
John 14:27c MEV

Here are a few resolution prayers for you to ponder. They are guaranteed to bring you the peace that passes all understanding (Philippians 4:7).

Help me, dear Father, to believe that you will provide for me this day. *"Whatever you ask for in prayer, with faith, you will receive." Matthew 21:22 NRSV*

Our Father, help me to hold fast to my faith in you. Give me strength and courage not to give up under pressure. *"He who overcomes will I make a pillar in the temple of My God" (Revelation 3:12 MEV). "Listen! I stand at the door and knock. If anyone hears my voice and opens the door, I will come in and dine with him, and he with Me" (Revelation 3:20 MEV).*

Father, help me be as gentle and kind to others as you have been with me. *"Blessed are the merciful: for they shall obtain mercy" (Matthew 5:7 MEV).*

Father God, send forth laborers into your harvest, and let me be the first one. *"Follow me, and I will make you fishers of men" (Matthew 4:19 MEV).*

Lord, lead me to someone who needs a friend. May I not be too busy to recognize your leading: *"There is no distinction between the Jew and the Greek: the same Lord is Lord of all is generous to all that call on him" (Romans 10:12 NRSV).*

My Lord and my God! I claim you as the Source and Object of my life. *"The Lord redeems the life of His servants, and all who take refuge in Him will not be punished"* (Psalm 34:22 *MEV*).

Let there be peace on earth and let it begin with me.

LET THERE BE PEACE ON EARTH

Words: Sy Miller and Jill Jackson
Music: Sy Miller and Jill Jackson; harm. By Charles H. Webb, 1987
© 1955, Assigned to Jan-Lee Music, © renewed 1983
United Methodist Hymnal, page 431

Let there be peace on earth, and let it begin with me;
Let there be peace on earth, the peace that was meant to be.
With God our creator, children all are we.
Let us walk with each other in perfect harmony.

Let peace begin with me; let this be the moment now.
With every step I take, let this be my solemn vow:
To take each moment and live each moment
in peace eternally.
Let there be peace on earth, and let it begin with me.

TRUE JOY—EVEN THOUGH

"Don't let your hearts be troubled. Believe in God, and believe also in me."
John 14:1 NRSV

It seemed that everything—my whole world—was falling down around me. Everywhere I turned, there was destruction and chaos. That was my world, and the outside world didn't look any better! People—innocent people—were being killed; floods were destroying people's homes and livelihoods; fires were raging and threatening towns; the government was threatening people instead of helping. Where was God? Didn't He care?

Jesus was asked the same thing in the boat that day on the Sea of Galilee, by his disciples, "Do you not care that we may drown?" (Matthew 8:23-26) He chided them for having little faith, and then He rose and commanded the waters to be still—and there was peace and there was quiet.

Where is Jesus in the midst of your troubles? He is right beside you, waiting for you to call upon Him—put your faith to work and trust Him. For you see, even in the midst of chaos, there is still joy—joy that no one nor any situation can steal from you when you are trusting in Jesus. Take your eyes off your problems—quit trying to solve it yourself—and put your hand in the hand of Jesus. He will raise you up.

There is a power in the name of Jesus that gives us strength, love, peace, and happiness. No love is greater than God's love.

Joy is spelled—**J**esus, **O**thers, and **Y**ou

Lord, help me rejoice and praise Your name even in the hard times. No matter how rough it gets, let me give thanks to the God of my salvation. Amen

Habakkuk 3:17-19 1Chronicles 16:23-27

LEFT BEHIND

"...we live by believing not by seeing." 2 Corinthians 5:7 NLT

Sometimes, Lord, it seems as though I've been left behind, especially concerning my family. I look at others who espouse such joy in their grandchildren and are included in the lives of their children. Then I hear others say that they are too close in proximity to their children and grandchildren—they know and see too much. Tell me, Lord, how do I deal with my sadness?

Being left behind is one thing, but feeling left behind is quite another. When Moses went up on the mountain to speak with God and left the people behind, they responded by getting into trouble. They thought they had lost the one who was guiding them through the desert, and they were left without their spiritual leader. They panicked! Why? They were people of little faith. They had no personal relationship with God!

Those who have a personal relationship with Jesus are never alone and they are never left behind. They simply go where God leads—sometimes up the mountain, sometimes down in the valley—but they do not go alone—God is always there with them.

When I feel alone or left behind, I remember that where the Holy Spirit leads, I will follow, and my family is always held close to my heart—He is with them, too.

Bless my soul, O Lord, and keep me and my family safe and at peace. Amen

2 Corinthians 5:7 Psalm 96:6 John 8:12 Psalm 36:9

COMPLAINING

"Do everything without complaining and arguing,"
Philippians 2:14 NLT

Sometimes life is like climbing up a mountain that never ends. Or it is like the bear that went over the mountain, and what did he see? He saw another mountain! Our struggles never seem to end; they pile up one upon another. It is so hard not to complain.

However, complaining to others doesn't make you feel better and it certainly doesn't make the other person feel good, either. Everyone has something going on in their own lives that is disturbing them as well. You say, but I need to let it out or I will explode!

There is one place, and one place only, to vent your complaints. The Lord, who is beside you and whose hand you hold as you walk up that mountain, is always ready to listen. Talk to Him and He will give you understanding and show you the way.

"For I have given rest to the weary and
joy to the sorrowing."
Jeremiah 31:25 NLT

Father, do your work in me. You know my heart and my desires; complete me and make me whole, living for You and not myself. Help me to be understanding. Give me strength where I am weak. Jesus, give me strength not to complain. Amen

Jeremiah 31:25 Philippians 2:14-15

DO NOT TAKE FOR GRANTED

"And the very hairs on your head are all numbered."
Luke 12:7 NLT

There are so many things that we take for granted: the rising and setting of the sun; the water will come out of the faucet when we turn the knob; the car will start when we turn the key; the morning will come; even our breathing. It is not until these things do not happen that we consider that they are finite and are dependent on a force much greater than you and I.

God has created and arranged this world, therefore He knows the intricacies of every element in it—even you and me. Taking for granted His ways puts us in great jeopardy of being fair game for the evil one, who is always waiting to get a foothold into our lives—even through the smallest crack.

Therefore, keep your eyes and ears open and give God the thanks and the Glory for each moment of the day and the happenings contained in each moment.

Dear Lord, I want to thank you for your unconditional love and for always being with me. I am never alone whether in the valleys of life or on the mountaintops. Your grace covers me and I am grateful. Amen

Luke 12:7 John 1:12 Acts 16:31 Romans 10:13

WHEN THINGS GO WRONG

"...give thanks for everything to God the Father in the name of our Lord Jesus Christ." Ephesians 5:20 NLT

My father once told me of an experience he had with the milk truck he was driving. In those days, the farmers put the milk from their cows in 30 gallon cans and picked up and brought to the creamery. My father drove one of those milk routes, which included going down the side of a mountain, through a village, and leveling out while crossing a bridge. One morning, the truck's brakes wouldn't hold; it rolled faster and faster through the village and its one red light; only slowing down as it leveled out after crossing the bridge!

Our lives can also get out of control—you feel as though you are racing down a downward slope. Soon you do not know which way to turn; you begin listening to people's complaints—and soon you do not even know who you are. But, there is hope—unlike the truck, you can put on your brakes.

Regardless of your situation, thank God, thank Him for His love; thank Him for everything. Call out the name of Jesus—He is waiting, longing for your recognition of His presence. Soon your life will begin to level out and you will experience peace as only Jesus can give you.

The right word at the right time! Because of God's unfailing love, my enemy, the devil, will NOT rejoice in my defeat! I need to live a life that will tell the world that I am a child of the light. Let me not hide my light under a bushel basket—let it shine! And do not let Satan blow it out—let it shine!

Psalm 13:3-5 Ephesians 5:20

THE PRESENCE

"...everyone who asks receives. Everyone who seeks, finds. And to everyone who knocks, the door will be opened."
Matthew 7:8 NLT

We were invited to someone's house for dinner. It was a place to which we had never been. We looked it up on the map and thought it would be no problem to find—the route looked pretty straight forward. Because of this, we were resolved not to use our GPS. All of a sudden, the road brought us to an intersection that we hadn't noticed on the map! We were forced to undo our resolve, swallow our pride, and ask for directions!

Our path through life is very similar. We think we know where we are going and are lured into a false sense of security; soon it is, "Oh well, life happens." We come to a crossroad and are unsure of which way to turn. We blindly wander down the path that seems right to us. What is the answer?

We have a Helper who knows the way—His name is the Holy Spirit. Jesus was born to die that He would go back to the Father, that He could send us His Holy Spirit (John 16:7). He is within us and all we need do is acknowledge His Presence and ask for His help. There is no weakness in asking—there is only strength because you know from whence your help comes.

Thank you, Lord, for your precious Holy Spirit sent to guide us daily. Amen

John 14:16-17 John 16:7 Zechariah 4:6 Matthew 7:7-8

Forgive me, Lord, for what I've done wrong. I humble myself before you as I give you thanks for your great sacrifice—You gave up Your life that I may live.

God, grant me the wisdom to come to you daily, to seek forgiveness for going against your will and to offer thanksgiving for Your Mercy and Grace. Grant me guidance through the power of Your Holy Spirit in the days to come. In Jesus' name I pray. Amen

Be anxious for nothing, but in everything, by prayer and supplication with gratitude, make your requests known to God. And the peace of God, which surpasses all understanding, will protect your hearts and minds through Christ Jesus.
Philippians 4:6, 7 MEV

THE ONE THING

"Whatever is good and perfect comes down to us from God our Father..."
James 1:17 NLT

Advertisements dominate the television, magazines, and newspapers. They tell us that we need this thing or that. Our lives won't be worth living if we aren't the proud owners of a new car, jewelry, or clothing. To live a full life, you need this kind of insurance or this particular medicine—"Just ask your doctor!" Our homes are full of "stuff" that we could very well do without.

It's a shame that we spend so much money on "things" that we don't really need, when the one and only thing we need doesn't cost a dime. It is something you can never lose and no one can take away from you. It is with you at all times. It is waiting for you to realize that there is a gift being offered and all you need do is accept it.

God is offering you His everlasting presence.

"[He] will be with you always, to the end of the age" (Matthew 28:20). NRSV

He promises to walk beside you and to carry you when you have a need.

You, O Lord, are the rock of my salvation—everything else is meaningless. Father, thank you for another day—teach me to be a doer of your word and not a hearer only. Amen

Psalm 62:5-8 Revelation 1:8 I Peter 2:9 James 1:17

UP FROM THE ASHES

"...when troubles come your way, consider it an opportunity for great joy."
James 1:2 NLT

Do you know that there is evil in the world? We read in the Book of Revelation that Satan and all his followers were thrown out of heaven. His followers, according to Revelation, were 1/3 of all the angels in heaven. Satan was once an Arch Angel who got too big for his britches and wanted to be God. In other words, he wanted to overthrow the throne! Where did he go? And what is he doing now?

He, and all the demons, are in the world! But bigger is He who is in you, than he who is in the world (I John 4:4).There is a spiritual battle going on in the midst of it (Ephesians 6:10-18). Do not worry, do not be afraid (Matthew 6:25-34) for through faith and believing and trust, God will deliver you and bring you up out the ashes and place you on a rock (Psalm 40:2).

Always remember to praise God in the midst of your trouble and suffering. Through each trial, you become equipped and receive courage to resist the evil one. In enduring various trials, your faith is strengthened. Remember who created this world and all it contains; the Creator will not allow His creation to be destroyed (Genesis 1).

Hang in there—God has already won the victory—Satan will not have the last word! Let the redeemed cry to the Lord who will bring you out of all your troubles.

James 1:2-4 Psalm 107:21-22

ENJOY THE PRESENT

"...for we walk by faith, not by sight."
2 Corinthians 5:7 NRSV

There are times that we wonder about our lives ahead of us. "How can I get through this terrible situation—divorce, death, surgery, class, abusive relationship, meeting, just this day!" you may wonder. There are many mountains that rise up that we may have to climb in the days ahead. It is like looking out of your hotel room at the peaceful valley below, but in the distance, you see a mountain that you may have to cross—not knowing what that mountain will entail, but you know you must get to the next peaceful valley.

When we focus on the mountain, we miss the joy of the peaceful valley. If and when we have to climb that mountain, our faith will give us the strength to do so. Paul writes,

"...for we walk by faith, not by sight"
(2 Corinthians 5:7 NRSV)

and encourages us to hold on tight to the Lord's hand as we walk our journey.

The truth is we cannot see beyond this moment, actually we only HAVE this moment, yesterday is gone and tomorrow may never come. But, it is true that God is with you and will help you through the storm.

Don't miss the blessing of today.

"Look to the Lord and his strength; seek his face always."
Psalm 105:4 (NIV)

Psalm 97:10   Psalm 18:29   Psalm 91:11-12

DOCTRINE OR DOGMA

"We must no longer be children, tossed to and fro and blown about by every wind of doctrine," Ephesians 4:14 NRSV

Stand firm, do not lose faith. Sometimes it is so easy to be led down the wrong path. Our "leaders" say things that sound so good, but are they? We trust their judgment and their words—without any further investigation—just blind trust. The question is are we following doctrine or dogma? Are we forgetting about our faith principles and simply listening to what someone else believes is true?

Isaiah warned the Hebrews of this very thing thousands of years ago; it has been true in every generation—even today. There is a danger in following human traditions rather than God's heart. We can end up modifying the Law to escape its authority! The writer of Proverbs writes: *"For I give you a good doctrine: Do not forsake My law." (4:2)*; and Jeremiah writes, *"A wooden idol is a worthless idol" (10:8)*.

Paul writes in Ephesians, *"We must no longer be children, tossed to and fro and blown about by every wind of doctrine"* (4:14). He writes about how we should live our new life in Christ, holding to its doctrines— *"Therefore be imitators of God, as beloved children, and live in love, as Christ loved us and gave himself up for us, a fragrant offering and sacrifice to God"(5:1)*.

Live your life, be pleasing to God, not men—for He is your salvation.

Mark 7:6-7 Hebrews 13:15 2 Corinthians 3:18
Psalm 73:23-24

KEEPING AN EYE

"...ask in faith never doubting." James 1:6a NRSV
"Lord, save me!" Matthew 14:30 NRSV

There will be many storms in this life—that is a given. But take courage, do not lose heart—*"You can do all things through Christ who strengthens you." Philippians 4:13*

When you read the story of Peter walking on the water (Matthew 18), you will notice that Peter could not do it on his own. He had to keep his eye on Jesus, not on the huge waves around him. This is also true for us. If we focus our attention on the problem, it will soon consume us and we will begin to sink in its negative energy. Instead, look to Jesus, and His positive energy will immediately bring you up out of the miry clay and set your feet upon a rock and put a song in your heart (Psalm 40:2-3).

The Psalmist gives us encouragement over and over again. David knew what it was like to run into trouble—even as he was following the Lord. The truth is that ole-sloo-foot is in a battle and wants you all to himself, but there is no salvation in him. Our only salvation is in the Lord who loves us, in spite of whatever trouble we may be in.

Call out, "Lord Jesus, save me!" He WILL answer, "Come." You, too, may walk on water. As the Lord spoke to Jeremiah, he speaks to you,

"Do not be afraid...I am with you to deliver you"
(Jeremiah 1:8).

Isaiah 43:18 Ephesians 2:6 Matthew 14:28-31

DIALOGUE

"Can all your worries add a single moment to your life"
Luke 12:25 NLT

Me: Good morning, Lord.
Lord: Good morning, my child.
Me: What a beautiful day you have blessed us with!
Lord: It is for your enjoyment, my child. Today is a new day—use it wisely.
Me: But, Lord, what about tomorrow? There are things I do not know—when we go to the place where we will offer our books and photos—what if the table isn't big enough? I mean, after all, we are being put in the hall! Maybe we should just stay home and forget about it. What a way to be treated!
Lord: Hush, hush—stop fretting. You are forgetting one thing—the most important thing—I will be there with you. It doesn't matter where you are—I will be there—even if you are in the basement. I will send people to you—trust me. Your job is to take care of today—continue with your preparations—do your work—I will prepare the way for tomorrow. In fact, I already have.
Me: Thank you, Lord. Prepare me to be a sanctuary for you.

When you worry about tomorrow, you miss the blessings of today.
God, give me inner strength that comes from You through Your Spirit. Thank you, Lord, for loving me so dearly.

Luke 12:22-26 Ephesians 3:20-21

OH, HOW I HAVE MISSED YOU

By
Rev. Betty A. Beach-Connell, 1985

The days and nights are but a blur
I have called out in the darkness
I have cried in the night.
O how I have missed you

Running, running
Work, busy work, piling up
People, people everywhere.
O how I have missed you

Walking in the beautiful field
Feeling the touch of the gentle breeze
Oh, so alone.
O how I have missed you

What is it that's missing?
I have family, I have friends
People, people everywhere.
O how I have missed you

What is it that's missing?
Solitude—peace
Away from the busyness.
O how I have missed you

The gift of silence
I heard your voice
I saw and felt you around me.
O how I have missed you

Ecstasy, what bliss
I have found you
I am back in the arms of my God.
O how I have missed you.

I am so glad I found you!

"BE STILL AND KNOW THAT I AM GOD."
Psalm 46:10 (NLT)

ACHIEVING SUCCESS

"...apart from me you can do nothing." John 15:5c NRSV

It is not a bad thing to want to do and be everything and all you can. The human condition calls us to want to be successful—it is how we achieve that success and what we do with it after we achieve it. The question is: Is our success worth it if we have lost our peace along the way?

The fact of the matter is God wants us to be successful. God's Word tells us in Jeremiah 29:11, *"For I know the plans I have for you...plans for good and not for disaster, to give you a future with hope."* It also says in Ephesians 2:14, *"For Christ himself has brought peace to us."* And in Psalm 37:4-5—*"Take delight in the Lord, and he will give you the desires of your heart. Commit everything you do to the Lord. Trust him and he will help you."*

So less may be more when you consider a life of peace in your soul against struggling to be what one might consider "on top of the heap." Success is trusting in God to show you the way. He will make you richer and more successful than all the kings of the world. Seek His face and trust the path on which He leads you—it will truly lead to a successful life.

When you give all the glory to God—God will glorify your life.

John 15:5 James 1:2-4

LIGHT SEPARATES

"Then God said, "Let there be light," and there was light." And God saw that the light was good. Then He separated the light from the darkness." Genesis 1:3-4 NLT

On my father's farm, after the cows were milked, the cans of milk were placed in the cooler. When they came out and were opened, the cream had separated from the milk and had risen to the top. Sometimes we would scoop some of the cream out to make whipped cream, but most times we would leave it there and stir it into the milk to make it richer. However, if you didn't keep it stirred, the cream would separate again.

God came into the world—He created the world—and His light separated the darkness. There was light because God is light. Before He graced us with His presence, we were in darkness. If we do not stay in close relationship with God, we become separated, just as the cream from the milk.

In God, there is no darkness at all (John 1:5); even the night becomes as day. God so ordered the universe that we would have time to do and time to rest—with God the darkness cannot overcome us—as long as we keep the cream stirred into the milk.

1 John 1:5-10 Psalm 32:8 Genesis 1:1

FORGIVENESS

"Forgive them Father for they know not what they do."
Luke 23:34 MEV

Do you mean you want me to forgive them after what they did to me? NEVER!!

We have all been hurt by someone; perhaps it was intentional, but many times it is not. But still we get all bent out of shape—understandably so.

It is at times like these that we must take a step back and be the bigger person. As a believer, there is no other place to go but to the Word of God for help. The one that hits me right between the eyes is *"Forgive as I have forgiven you"* (Matthew 6:12). I remember all the things I have done that have hurt others and, thereby, hurt my Lord—and, yet, I am forgiven <u>and</u> absolved. I have been set free of all sin and guilt through the life-giving act of Jesus who died upon the cross for my atonement and was resurrected to prove that there was new life to be lived.

Forgiveness does not say that you condone or accept what has been done—it says that you are releasing the burden to the One who can take care of it. You are laying your burden down to the One whose yoke is easy. You can put your shoulders back, raise your head up, and respond with love. Who knows what changes this will bring to you and the ones who have wronged you!

Jesus looked beyond our faults and saw our need and showered His grace upon us.

Thank you, Lord, for dressing me with the clothing of salvation and spreading a table before me in the presence of my enemies. Amen

Colossians 3:13 Isaiah 61:10 Romans 5:5

LISTEN TO ME AND OPEN YOU HEARTS

"Any who believes in me may come to me and drink! For the scriptures declare, 'Rivers of living water will flow from his heart.'" John 7:38 NLT

The Lord blessed us with 5 senses—the sense of smell, taste, touch, sight, and hearing. Therefore, we can "smell the roses," taste the food we eat; touch the little baby and feel their softness; see the beauty of God's creation; and, if we believe, hear God's still, small voice calling to us from amidst the chaos of the world.

Sometimes we can't believe what we see, as Moses when he saw the bush burning and it was not consumed. When he stopped and looked closer, he heard the voice of God. Something like that does not compute with our limited knowledge, but look closer and listen. God may be speaking to you. When it looks too good to be true, look closer; God may be trying to get your attention.

You see, we can hear with more than our ears; we can hear with our hearts. If you open your heart to the voice of the Holy Spirit, and listen to His voice, He will empower you to follow His calling. The Holy Spirit's home [temple] is your body, and He fills your heart with compassion and love.

When you come to a train crossing, you must stop, look, and listen—not doing so may result in a tragedy. The same is true of not stopping and looking and listening to the voice of God on your journey through life.

Exodus 3:5 1Corinthians 6:19 John 7:38-39

THE QUIET

"In quietness and trust is your strength." Isaiah 30:15 NRSV

"It's a jungle out there," Mr. Monk used to say on his weekly TV program. He was scared of everything, especially germs. But, at the same time, he had an obsession to touch everything he passed by! He was superstitious and wouldn't step on the cracks in the sidewalk. He was a prisoner to his fears. Where could he get help?

Isaiah writes: *"For thus said the Lord God…In returning and rest you shall be saved; in quietness and in trust shall be your strength."* (30:15 NRSV)

Sometimes, we can make a mess out of our lives, and there seems to be nowhere that we can get relief or help. But our Lord always stands ready if we would reach out to Him. He says, *"Behold, I stand at the door knocking, if anyone opens the door I will come in and eat with them"* (Revelation 3:20). Christ is knocking on the door of your heart—you are the one who must open the door and invite Him in.

When Jesus comes into your heart, rest in His presence; allow the quiet to embrace you and feel the brush of angel's wings on your cheeks and the breath of the Holy Spirit to fill your lungs, as God breathes new life into your soul.

Lord, continue to let Your light shine through me. Teach me to apply Your word in my daily life.

Psalm 116:5-7 Ephesians 5:20 Isaiah 30:15

SETBACKS OR OPPORTUNITIES

"The steps of man are made firm by the Lord; He delights in his way." Psalm 37:23 MEV

What am I going to do? I don't know which way to turn! I've gotten everything prepared—I've spent hours and hours getting ready—and now we can't go!?!

We had spent weeks and weeks preparing, crafting, and making items for the craft show. Our space was reserved and our fee was paid. Then it happened—disaster struck and there was no way we were going to be able to make it! We had made our plans, but God is now directing our path. (Proverbs 16:9)

We could have moaned and groaned; anger and disappointment could've taken over our every waking moment, but instead, a sort of peace and release settled over us as we prayed, "God, whatever it is You want us to do, we will do."

What we thought to be a setback turned out to be an opportunity—it has shown us a much better way. The preparations gave our life meaning as we shared those moments together. The products became a symbol of our love for each other and the decisions to skip the craft show became a blessing as we waited in anticipation for God's direction of our path.

"Commit your actions to the Lord, and your plans will succeed." Proverbs 16:3 NLT

Help me, Lord, to continue to press toward the mark of the higher calling which is Christ Jesus. Help me to stay focused and not grow weary. I pray for everyone to strive to do the will of God and see the results. Fall sometimes we will, but when we get back up, we will know we are covered by the blood of Jesus. Thank you, Jesus. Amen

Colossians 4:2 Philippians 3:7-9a

WALK—DO NOT RUN (OR SKIP)

"...everything will be fine with you." Exodus 33:14b NLT

I remember playing the game of Hop Scotch. We would draw boxes on the sidewalk/concrete—2 boxes, 1 box, 2 boxes, etc.—until we had enough for 1-10. In each box, we would put a number—then we took our pottsy (which was usually a smooth rock or can lid) and starting with number 1, threw it and hoped it would land flat on its mark. Then we had to jump over that box and land our feet squarely in the rest—turn around—come back—pick up the pottsy—jump over the box, and do it all over again with number 2,3,4 and so on

This game taught me self-control—there were times when my pottsy would miss its mark or I would touch the ground when I shouldn't have, causing me to lose my turn. If the game wasn't played in the right spirit, one could become angry, disappointed, or hurt. This is much like the game of life—we must play it in the right attitude and with the right Spirit.

We cannot hop, skip, or jump our way through life. We must walk, and sometimes stop and wait, to follow the path that God has planned for each of us. We tend to forget, sometimes, that it is all in God's hands—and He holds us in His palm. There are times when things seem to move so quickly that we miss the box, or the task seems so daunting that our pottsy doesn't seem to hit its mark, but through all of this, God is saying, "...I will go with you...everything will be fine with you."

Dear Lord, fill me with Your Grace as I prepare for the task that is before me. Do not let me stray from Your Presence, O Lord. Lock me in the sheepfold that I may walk in peace—may others be attracted to Your light and be blessed.

Exodus 33:14 Deuteronomy 33:25 Hebrews 13:20-21

THE MAGNET

"...I am with you, and will protect you wherever you go."
Genesis 28:15 MEV

In my childhood, I had many toys to keep me busy. They were ones with which I had to use my imagination. I especially loved my paper dolls. I would sit for hours, cutting out the figures and the clothes that went with them. Then there was the jumping bean. When you placed it in the palm of your hand, it would seemingly roll and jump all by itself. Also, I fondly remember the Scotty dogs. One was white and one was black and each had a magnet attached to their feet. When you put them together right, they would cling to each other, but if not, they would repel each other. I'd put one on top of a piece of paper and one underneath, upside down. I'd move one and the other would either follow or run in the opposite direction. The choice was mine—to stay together or move apart. I would giggle and giggle as the dogs moved about.

God is like that magnet. Once we get connected, form a relationship, and accept Jesus into our hearts, He promises to never, ever leave us. Wherever we go—He is! Eventually, as our relationship grows stronger, there will be nowhere we will want to be, except on the path that God has chosen for us.

There will be times when you may make a choice that will cause you to repel from God's grasp—but He is never out of sight and will always be calling you back, for God's love is like a magnet.

There is no place we can go where the presence of the Lord will not be.

Philippians 4:12,19   Genesis 28:15   Romans 8:38-39

SEEK MY FACE

"...it is impossible to please God without faith."
Hebrews 11:6NLT

This morning, I looked in the mirror and saw someone who didn't know what to do. The reflection revealed a face that was lost. Where do I go? Where do I turn? What do I say? How can I fix this? I breathed, "Please, Jesus, help me—help them. I wish I could wave a magic wand and make it all right!" But, the truth is, I can't!

Trouble and discord have reared their ugly heads once again! This happens so often in families—mine is not the only one. What people usually do is ignore it and it dies down, but it will eventually rise up again, usually at the most inopportune time when it can do the most damage.

I heard God's voice saying, "Trust me, obey me, I am with you." I breathed, "Jesus." Then I knew. It is not up to me to "fix" this or any other situation. It is up to the ones involved, it is their responsibility. My job is to remind them—that is all. I will pray and God will be present with them as they sort through the maze of rebuilding their relationship. I will pray that their relationship will develop into a friendship filled with love—never to be broken. My faith tells me this is possible because all things are possible with God.

The greatest lesson we can learn is to love God with all our heart, mind, and soul and love each other as ourselves.

Dear Lord, teach us to fully open our hearts to you that your love may fill us. Help us to allow the Holy Spirit to breathe His power into our beings and work through us to bring about reconciliation and peace. Amen

John 8:29 Hebrews 11:5-6 Psalm 37:4

BLOWING BUBBLES

"Can all your worries add a single moment to your life?"
Luke 12:25 NLT

We were out in the courtyard blowing bubbles. After dipping the wand in the bubble solution, I put it in front of my mouth and gently blew on the film that covered the opening in the wand. Almost like magic, a bubble began to form; it would detach itself and gently float off in the breeze.

Watching my bubbles float around, seemingly without a care in the world, gave me pause. I started to think about the steps that I take each day. Were they like these bubbles? Do my steps take on the air of peace and tranquility? I must admit, sometimes my fears about my next step debilitates me—and I miss a blessing and I become more like a frightened child than one who knows their Protector.

The truth is, all this worry cannot add to your life; it can only take away from it. The Holy Spirit is within you—He has been from the moment of conception—He is there to encourage and assist you—all you have to do is acknowledge His presence. He is the one who puts the wind beneath your wings and the air in your bubble.

You are that bubble that floats about in peace and tranquility when you know the One who breathes life into your soul. Just like that bubble couldn't become a bubble until I blew into it, your life cannot be all it was meant to be until the Holy Spirit is invited in and breathes the breath of life into you.

My faith tells me that my God will supply all my needs.

Luke 12:22-26 Deuteronomy 31:6 Genesis 2:7

THIS IS A GOOD DAY

*"Happy are those who...walk in the
light of your presence, Lord"*
Psalm 89:15 NLT

Today is a good day to be a good day.

When you walk in the presence of the Lord, knowing that He goes before you, there can be nothing but good—even if tragedy strikes. Like a little child crossing the street in the middle of traffic, holding his father's hand, you will make it. All you have to do is hold on to the Father's hand.

If this seems too simplistic, it is! When you walk through the storms of life—and you will walk <u>through</u> them—you are not alone. Jesus is there walking with you. Sometimes He protects you from the storm and sometimes He allows the storm to overtake you—at least, temporarily—but you should never let go of His hand. As a child must be disciplined from time to time so that they can be the best that they can be, so to you who are believers. The child's parents never leave them; your God will never leave you.

This is a good day because God is with you. This is a good day because when all is said and done, nothing can separate you from the love of Jesus Christ, which is more precious than gold. Say to yourself, <u>"I am going to have a good day!"</u>— then trust in God with all your heart.

Dear God, help me to trust in you. I know you hold me in the palm of your hand—help me to rest in the comfort of your presence. Amen

Psalm 89:15-16 I John 3:19-20 Jude 24-25 Psalm 41:12

THE SECRET

"...And this is the secret; Christ lives in you."
Colossians 1:27b NLT

I'm sure you were asked many times if you could keep a secret. And if you said, "Yes," the person went on to tell you something that they wanted no one else to know—probably something very personal. Then again, they might have told you because they knew you would tell someone else—sort of reverse psychology.

Well, what I am about to tell you is a secret that has been hidden far too long! God created the world and breathed life into it (Genesis 1, 2). It was meant to be a Paradise of great joy, but that Paradise was invaded by sin (Genesis 3). From then on, God's people were unable to live an obedient life unto the Lord. Finally, God came to earth in the flesh—He was called Jesus—born a baby in a manger. This baby grew in stature and wisdom among us. John 1 says, *"The Word became flesh and the Word was God..."* But we put Him to death and still He rose and lives forever in Heaven at the right hand of God. But He did not leave us alone—He left His Holy Spirit to guide us and live within us.

This has been kept a secret far too long, it must be told. This secret is one that will fill you with joy—regardless of the circumstances you may be facing. It will give you strength to face the future—because Christ Jesus lives!

Now let us tell everyone about Christ who is the visible image of the invisible God, using all the wisdom God has given us to teach them about a perfect relationship with Christ Jesus.

Don't keep the Good News a secret—spread the word.

"May the God of hope fill you with all joy and peace in believing, so that you may abound in hope by the power of the Holy Spirit." *Romans 15:13 NRSV*

Colossians 1:27 Isaiah 42:6 Nehemiah 8:10 Romans 15:13

Lord, I pray that you give me wisdom and understanding of your word and that your will be done in my life that I may glorify You. No matter what the day may bring, direct my thoughts to You, Father that I may always walk in your light. You are the light unto my path. In Jesus' name I pray. Amen

"See, I have inscribed you on the palms of my hands;"
Isaiah 49:16 MEV

THE MAZE

"...You have held me by my right hand..." Psalm 73:23b MEV

It is autumn, and this is the season of the corn maze. When going through this maze, it is difficult to know which way to turn—every turn looks the same. It is difficult to know which way is out. Getting lost in a maze can give you an awful fright!

When you think about it, life is very much like a corn maze. When traveling down the road of life, there are many turns and detours that you must make. It can be difficult to know which way is the right one, and just when you think you've made the right choice—it's not!

"How can I know the right path?" you may ask. The more you think about it, the more confusing it gets. "Which way do I choose?" Well, asking other people doesn't always help, because they are calling on their own experiences—what has worked for them may not work for you. But, there is a way—where there seems to be no way, God will make a way.

Come to the Lord in prayer. He knows which road you should choose because He has planned your path long ago. Bow your head, ask Him, then be patient—He will show you the way. You will see your way clearly and be at peace—in His time.

"Listen! I am standing at the door, knocking; if you hear my voice and open the door, I will come in to you and eat with you, and you with me." Revelation 3:20NRSV

No matter what the day may bring, I will hold on to the Lord's right hand. He will lead me through the maze and fog; He will keep me from stumbling.

Psalm 73:23-24 I Corinthians 13:12

BLESSINGS OF THORNS

"...and remember, I am with you always, even to the end of the age."
Matthew 28:20 NRSV

Recently I read without the thorns, we cannot have roses. When we buy a dozen roses at a flower shop, usually there are no thorns, but the thorns were there before the beautiful roses. Take a look at your rose bushes at home—there are thorns before the roses.

There are thorns in our lives, also. I wonder how many of us think about being thankful for those thorns. Perhaps, the thorns (the trials and tribulations) in our lives are responsible for the roses (the good times) that occur. Should we not give thanks for the thorny times? For without them, we may not experience the joy of the blessings of happy days.

Jesus appeared to the disciples in the midst of their despair and proclaimed peace for them. He will do the same for you. Give God thanks; remember He has promised to never leave you nor forsake you. Also, we cannot have an Easter unless we have a Good Friday. The grave could not contain our Lord; He arose and lives with us yet today. Man tried to kill Him, but God came to His rescue—He will do the same for you—if you BELIEVE.

Give thanks with a grateful heart for each and every day, whether it contains thorns or roses. You see, God is always with us through thick and thin, whether it is a stormy or sunny day, and even in the thick of thorns.

Luke 24:3b Hebrews 13:15 John 20:1-10

KEEP FOCUSED

*"This is the day the Lord has made,
we will rejoice and be glad in it."
Psalm 118:24 MEV*

The stage was dark. There are props and actors placed in various places—you know they are there, but you cannot see them. You sit in the audience in silence—in the dark—and wait. Suddenly a spotlight comes on and focuses on one lone actor who begins to sing. The props and other actors are but shadows. As the actor who is singing moves about, the spotlight follows—as it does, it reveals more shadowy figures. A commotion arises somewhere on stage, but the actor in the spotlight continues singing and keeps his focus.

Those who are believers in Christ Jesus and walk in the light of His Word can also move and live and have their being surrounded in peace. Even though you live in a chaotic world; suffer losses; and do battle with all sorts of tragedies, you too can continue on unscathed because God holds you in His spotlight. God will not allow your foot to stumble; the arrows of the evil one will only fall by your side (Psalm 91).

When you give thanks and praise to God for all things, the door is open to peace and happiness. Pray and open your heart to God who loves you—unconditionally. Keep your focus on God and His creation and the things of this world will grow strangely dim.

Prayer and thanksgiving to our God are the keys to a peaceful soul.

Psalm 116:17 Colossians 3:15 Acts 9:18 Revelation 19:3-6
Psalm 100:4-5

HIGHER THAN THE SKY—
DEEPER THAN THE OCEAN

"Cast all your cares upon Him; because He cares for you."
I Peter 5:7 NRSV

"Let them praise the Lord for His goodness and His wonderful works to the people!" Psalm 107: 8, 15, 21 MEV

Sometimes we find ourselves wandering around in the wilderness just as the Hebrew people were, having fled from the torture of slavery by the Egyptians. The Syrians today are fleeing from persecution, looking to be free to live their lives peacefully. All three—you, the Hebrews, and the Syrians—have been given the same opportunity to overcome. His name is Jesus.

Jesus, God in the flesh, can lead you to safety and peace. Just call upon His name—whether you shout it or whisper it or it is said silently in your heart—He will hear and answer. Just as the word of the Lord came to Jeremiah, it will come to you.

"Call to Me, and I will answer you, and show you great and might things which you do not know." Jeremiah 33:3 MEV
"Today if you hear His voice, do not harden your hearts," Hebrews 4:7b/Psalm 95:7b MEV

God loves you in a way that you cannot comprehend. His love is higher than the sky and deeper than the ocean. Once you open your heart to Him, you will understand the expanse of His love for you. He stands before you saying:

"Peace be with you...my peace I give to you, not as the world gives,"
John 20:19/John 14:27 MEV

He offers you perfect and lasting peace. Do you not see it?

Ephesians 3:16-19 Psalm 107:21-22

MR. FIXIT

"I will instruct you and teach you in the way you should go;"
Psalm 32:8 MEV

Have you watched a TV show entitled "Mr. Fix-it?" The concept is to show you that you can fix anything! And, not only that, it is easy! It is good to know how to fix things that are broken—there is no doubt about that—but everything!?!

Perhaps this is true of material things, but what about situations in life—can we always fix those on our own? Some think they must fix every situation that comes to their attention, but the reality is we cannot. But do not fret; be faithful and take your requests to God through Jesus Christ. He will give you the peace that passes all understanding (Philippians 4:6-7). Remember that where there seems to be no way, God will make a way.

Do you have something troubling you? Do you wish you could fix it and make all things right again? Maybe you wish you could go back and do something over again. Maybe you have a family member who is in trouble and you just know you could fix it if you were there. Whatever it is, if you believe, God will make it right, but only in His time. Whatever it is, take it to the Lord in prayer—He will show you the way—for there is only one thing that is needed and that is to sit at the feet of Jesus and worship Him.

Isaiah 58:11 Isaiah 40:11 Luke 10:41-42 Philippians 3:20-21

A CANOPY

"...His compassions do not fail. They are new every morning..."
Lamentations 3:22b-23a MEV

Sitting in your camper or outside your tent, on a crisp, fresh morning, watching the rising sun, can be an awesome experience. As you experience the warmth of the sun, your ears pick up the sounds of nature—it is as though a great symphony orchestra is playing a good morning song. Somewhere in the distance, though, you hear a rumble of thunder (the Tympani's are playing) and the clouds begin to roll in. Soon the rain begins to fall and you retreat to the cover of your camper or tent—it is a canopy of safety and protection. You trust that it will keep you dry, warm and safe; you wait for the storm to pass.

The storms of life roll in unexpectedly, too. In the midst of a beautiful day, "stuff" happens to change the tide. What do we do? Where do we go for protection and safety? How can we know the way?

You have a canopy that is always available; it is a banner over you and it will never fail. Believing in the Goodness, Mercy, and Love of God through Christ Jesus is a covering through which nothing can penetrate—it is impenetrable—if you believe. David cried out to the Lord in his distress;

"Make me know your ways, O Lord, teach me Your paths."
Psalm 25:4

"Keep me safe 'til the storm passes by.
'Til the storm passes over, 'Til the thunder sounds no more,
"Til the clouds roll forever from the sky
Hold me fast, let me stand in the hollow of Thy hand;
Keep me safe 'til the storm passes by."
('Til the Storm Passes By—words and music by Mosie Lister)

Psalm 25 Lamentations 3:22-26

BULLIES

"...the battle belongs to the Lord," I Samuel 17:47 MEV

People who threaten and take advantage of those who are seemingly weaker than they are nothing but bullies and, therefore, cowards. Just think, if they would turn all that energy they are putting into their acts of violence around, what this world could be! There is hope, however, even for those who commit these horrible acts of violence. Where does help come from? It comes from the Lord who never gives up on his people—the people give up on the Lord.

"My help comes from the Lord, who made heaven and earth." Psalm 121:2

What bigger bully could there be than Goliath, the giant, who was a Philistine and threatened the Hebrews? Yet, all the armies couldn't stop them; it took a little shepherd boy, David, who took the name of the Lord and stood up to Goliath. He looked this bully straight in the eye and stopped him dead in his tracks!

The battle we face today against bullies and terrorists is not a physical battle, it is a spiritual one. It is one that ultimately will be won by those who believe and call upon the name of the Lord—just as David did. We can conquer evil if we remain faithful to God's Word and follow the steps of Jesus. For there is strength and power to overcome in His name.

"Not by might nor by power, but by my Spirit says the Lord of Hosts." Zechariah 4:6

Ephesians 6:12 Philippians 2:9-11

HOVERING

"Surely the Lord is in this place, and I did not know it."
Genesis 28:16 MEV

Looking out across the pond, we saw an Osprey hovering over the water. Then in an instant the bird dove toward the water and back up. It had caught a fish in its talons. Flying off with its family's meal, I can imagine its satisfaction. People have figured out how to duplicate a bird's hovering—we call them drones. Drones are a new phenomenon that in some cases are causing havoc because they are not used properly, but they have a good potential.

Perhaps, this is not a good analogy, but if you think of a drone, and the way it works, you may be able to understand the presence of God. God's presence is always with us. His Holy Spirit is hovering close enough so that He can be with you in an instant when you call upon Him. No matter what the circumstance, no matter what you may or may not have done, God's promise remains:

"I will never leave you nor forsake you." Hebrews 13:5 MEV

Though you may not see Him, He is hovering—He is as close as a heartbeat—waiting for you to turn to Him.

"Remember, I am with you, and I will protect you wherever you go...For I will not leave you until I have done what I promised you." Genesis 28:15 MEV

Psalm 31:20 Genesis 28:11-16

THE PERFECT FIT

"In Him you...were sealed with the promised Holy Spirit."
Ephesians 1:13 MEV

We are always looking for the perfect fit. Whether it be clothing, property, or a relationship, nothing will suffice, but a perfect fit. The striving for perfection is burdensome and sometimes destructive—but when it is found, it is heavenly.

You may downplay the need for perfection by saying, "Nobody's perfect. I'm not perfect, you are not perfect." But then, you give in to that small voice you hear in your head that tells you "I can't" or "I'm not worth it." **DO NOT LISTEN TO THAT VOICE!** God says you are loved and He will provide all your needs. It is His love that is the "perfect fit" and will make all your days right for you.

There are things that you do not know and things that are invisible to your eye, but if you have faith, your heart can see. Clothes can be tried on and kept or discarded, depending upon the fit. Relationships sometimes do not work—do not be afraid—God will clothe you with His love and He will lead you to the right relationship, if you will ask Him.

"Do not fear, you are more valuable than many sparrows."
(Matthew 10:31) Therefore, God **WILL** take care of you.

Matthew 10:29-31 Hebrews 11:27 2 Corinthians 4:18
Philippians 4:19
Colossians 3:2-3

HOPE

"So after Abraham had patiently endured, he obtained the promise."
Hebrews 6:15 MEV

> Hope—an attitude toward the future, as assurance that God's promises will be kept, a confidence that what is bad will pass and what is good will be preserved.

Hope of heaven. As Christians, followers of Jesus and His teachings, this is our hope—the hope of heaven. It is not a hope to die—as some think—it is a hope to live! Jesus has shown us the way to life eternal. But, some, like Thomas, ask the question, "How can we know the way?"

Live as though heaven is on earth.

There can be no other way to live a life of peace than through hope. Hope helps us to wait patiently for the promise that God has made, to all who have faith, of everlasting life with Him. We can live that life here on earth as we demonstrate God's love—in good times and bad. Hope is our help, our stabilizer.

Jesus has gone on before us and waits for the day that we will join Him behind the veil in the Holy place called Heaven. The Bible tells us this story beginning in Genesis and ending with Revelation. God comes to us in the midst of great tribulation, great trials, great sorrow, and in times of great joy. Your hope, which builds out of your faith, is your salvation, in that it allows your heart and mind to become aware of the presence of God.

"Now may the God of hope fill you with all joy and peace in believing, so that you may abound in hope, through the power of the Holy Spirit." Romans 15:13

Romans 8:23-25 Hebrews 6:18-20

NO LIMITS
"There is therefore no condemnation for those who are in Christ Jesus,"
Romans 8:1 MEV

Question—"Do you think women can be pastors?" Response—"If God can use a teenage virgin to bear His Son, then why can He not use a woman to deliver His message?"

There are no limits with God, and there is no condemnation in Jesus. God created man and He created woman—How?—in His image. He created them to be helpmates. He calls us to be His children who follow His Word—ALL OF US, no restrictions on gender, race, creed, economics, age, cultural, handicaps, or any other differences we might expound.

We are part of the family of God. As such, we each have a role to play; without any one of us, the family wouldn't be complete. Therefore, we do the work that God calls us to do, to complete the beautiful picture painted by the Holy Spirit.

God calls some of us to be apostles, some prophets, some evangelist, some pastors, and some teachers (Ephesians 4:11) for a distinct purpose—*"The building up of the body of Christ..."* With God all things are possible"(Matthew 19:26)—even Pastors who are women!

The question is—Do you believe in the sovereignty of God? If your answer is "Yes," then you know there are no limits to the way God works with those whom He has chosen (John 15:16).

Romans 8:1 Ephesians 4:11-13 Matthew 19:26 Genesis 1:21 John 16:16 Isaiah 55:5

"If I take the wings of the morning and dwell at the end of the sea, even there Your hand shall guide me, and Your right hand shall take hold of me."
Psalm 139:9, 10 *MEV*

EYES AND EARS

*"...your eyes shall see your Teacher.
Your ears shall hear a word behind you..."*
Isaiah 30:20-21 MEV

Many years ago, when waiting for the main feature in a movie theater, there would be news reports on the screen. Before the reports began, an image would appear of the world with a back voice saying, "This is the eyes and the ears of the world." We could then see and hear the story. Today the eyes and ears of the world have expanded due to technology.

As we journey through this life on earth, we experience many hurdles and pitfalls, but we must never lose hope and always keep the faith. For each stumble, hurdle, and pitfall has contained within it a teachable moment.

We see the terrible circumstance or tragedy and feel the grief and pain and struggle. But somewhere deep inside, if we concentrate and look beyond our problems, we can also hear the voice that will comfort, guide, and direct us to safety and peace. That voice may or may not be audible, but the ears of our heart will hear. You will hear your Savior speaking,

"This is the way, walk in it" (Isaiah 30:21 MEV).

Remember all things are temporary EXCEPT God's love for you—that is Eternal.

God is our eyes and ears of the world—listen closely and you will hear his back voice, too.

II Corinthians 4:6-7 Matthew 5:3:6 Psalm 150

AWARENESS

"Come to Me, all you who labor and are heavily burdened, and I will give you rest." Matthew 11:28 MEV

During my school days, my teachers would reprimand us by telling us to "pay attention and try harder!" In the workplace, if we do not continually strive to do better, it is possible that someone will surpass us and we might even lose our job. In a relationship (some of them, at least), if we slack off or become complacent, that relationship may fail. But, you see, the world deals with us on a different level than God.

"Greater is He that is in you, than He who is in the world."
I John 4:4 MEV

The fact of the matter is, and this is what we need to understand, that God's love for us is unconditional! When we confess our belief in God's one and only Son, Jesus, and profess our love for Him, we are forever and always under the protection of God—no holds barred!

The times that we feel disconnected or far away from God is because our awareness of God's loving presence feigned. It is precisely at these times that we need to turn our eyes upon Jesus, acknowledging that He is the one who can and will bring us back into the fullness of His presence, as we see Him more fully.

I John 4:15-18 Deuteronomy 33:27

"O soul, are you wearied and troubled?
No light in the darkness you see?
There's light for a look at the Savior,
and life more abundant and free!
Turn your eyes upon Jesus, look full in His wonderful face,
And the things of this earth will grow strangely dim
In the light of His glory and grace.
(Words and music by Helen H. Lemmel, 1922)

Let us make this commitment—

"I for my part confide in Your kindness; may my heart exult in Your salvation!" Psalm 13:5 MEV

LESS IS MORE

"You did not choose Me, but I chose you...
go and bear fruit..."
John 15:16 MEV

There was a charming television commercial in which four or five small children and one adult sat around a child-size table. The adult asked the children, "What would you like more of?" One by one they answered—the adult listened intently with great interest. Then one little girl spoke with much emphasis and expression about how less is more and if you had more, it really would be less. When she finished, the adult simply said, "I understand."

Perhaps that is where we all should be—step back and understand that sometimes less is more. We tend to run ourselves ragged doing things. We seem to think the more we do, the better we will be—the better we will be seen by others. As a result, we only succeed in getting ourselves burned out, unable to function.

God has chosen you to bear fruit, but not in all the trees! He chose you to spread His word and love and brighten the corner where He has planted you. Take time to be with Him and you will see that less is really more as He shows you each day the way He has for you. When you bloom where you are planted, a beautiful garden will grow and others will see God's goodness.

"I can do all things because of Christ who strengthens me."
Philippians 4:13 MEV

Isaiah 64:4 John 15:5 Psalm 36:9

FEAR VS JOY

"I will both lie down in peace and sleep; for You, Lord, make me dwell safely and securely." Psalm 4:8 MEV

Do not let fear steal your joy! Search for those things that bring peace to your heart. There are many more blessings in a day than things to fear. All we have to do is set our minds on those things. As Paul says,

"...whatever things are true, whatever things are just, whatever things are pure, whatever things are lovely, whatever things are of good report; if there is any virtue, and if there is any praise, think on these things." Philippians 4:8 NRSV

It is true our news reports are full of murder, terrorism, and such. They would have you believe that we all should stay in our homes to be safe, but even then there is no guarantee. Only occasionally and briefly do we see and/or hear of some wonderful, up-lifting story that makes our heart sing for joy.

God speaks to us through the storm; His still, small, but ever-present voice assures us that He is here in the midst. He will surely protect us, securing our future with Him. He calls us not to lose hope—to hold on to our faith—and never cease in our commitment to love Him and one another. He will take care of the rest. May the joy of the Lord live in your heart!

"May the God of hope fill you with all joy and peace as you trust in him, so that you may overflow with hope by the power of the Holy Spirit."
Romans 15:13 (NIV)

Psalm 46:1-3 Psalm 89:15

IN LOSING YOU ARE FOUND

"Look all things have become new."
II Corinthians 5:17c MEV

Leo Tolstoy says, "In our end is our beginning" (paraphrased). Tolstoy ended his life as a Communist and began a new life as a Christian. He saw his life in a new and glorious light. He saw the world differently, as well as those around him. Everything was bathed in the light of Christ, but did it make things easier for him? NO! In some ways, it made it more difficult. But, in the end, his decision would save him for all eternity!

When we lose ourselves to the Lord, we ultimately find the "you" that our Lord meant us to be. When Paul said to the church at Corinth,

"Everything old has passed away; see everything has become new"
(II Corinthians 5:17cMEV)

he wasn't referring to the fact that the circumstances have changed or disappeared. He was saying that the way the person looks at and responds to them has changed, which in the end, will change the situation. He was saying that they now know that they have a helper by their side at all times; they were not alone.

This is the message for each of us—lose yourself in God's love and you will find peace, joy, and, most of all, love.

Ephesians 2:10 I John 4:7-8 John 15:4

AN ADVENTURE

"See, I will do a new thing...shall you not be aware of it?"
Isaiah 44:19 MEV

Each year we begin anew. Of course, we know that nothing has really changed. We can't treat our lives as though we were ripping a page out of a book. For some, the first day of the year is a blue one, as they come down from the excitement of the New Year's Eve gala celebrations. We can talk ourselves into a false sense of security, telling ourselves that our troubles are over—tomorrow everything will be different.

The fact is, tomorrow—no, today—can be different—you can be different. Take a new view on life by recognizing that there is a higher authority—higher than any government—that can lead you toward a new beginning. His name is Jesus. God sent Himself to us in the flesh so that we would understand that He lives.

What an exciting adventure when we turn our lives over to the Lord! Close your eyes, concentrate on His beauty and love, invite Him into your heart, breathe in the presence of the Holy Spirit—now open your eyes and see yourself as a new creation. Begin again, holding the hand of Jesus, "Do you not perceive it?"

"I am about to do a new thing; now it springs forth,
do you not perceive it?"
Isaiah 43:19 NRSV

Romans 12:2 Jeremiah 29:11-12

REFRESHMENT

"Seek the Lord and His strength; seek His presence continuously." Psalm 105:4 MEV

Fear not at what a day may bring. You have been promised a Helper who will guide you through each second, minute, hour, day, week, and year. Open your heart to Him and He will refresh your soul and give you strength to face even the toughest challenges.

There are many forms of refreshment: A cold glass of water on a warm day; a hot bath to ease sore muscles; a conversation with a loved one; or snuggling by the fire on a cold night; etc. These things, and many others, are refreshing to the body and allow you to relax—for a while—but soon it is the same ole, same ole.

The advice Jesus gave to Martha is apropos for us today. Martha saw her sister, Mary's, act of worship as something that was interfering with the work that had to be done. But Jesus corrected her by telling her that worshipping her Lord was paramount to getting the work done (Luke 10:39-42). In other words, worshipping, praising, and being in the Lord's presence must come first!

Giving the Lord undivided attention doesn't take away from your day—it adds to it! Sitting at the feet of Jesus—being in His presence—is refreshment for your soul that will carry you through your day.

> Fear not on what a day may bring.
> Only one thing is needful,
> That is to sit at the feet of Jesus
> And pour out your love for Him.
>
> Psalm 27:7-8 Luke 10:39-42 (TEV)

IS IT I?

"Then they began to ask one another, which one of them it could be who would do this." Luke 22:23 MEV

"They began to be sorrowful and to say to Him one by one, "Is it I?" and another, "Is it I?" Mark 14:19 MEV

The twelve who had been His inner circle, and had been with Him constantly for three years, were gathered with Him around the table. He had been telling them strange things like,

"I have eagerly desired to eat this Passover with you before I suffer." (Luke 22:15)

The twelve had depended upon Jesus for everything—they couldn't bear to be without Him. Every moment that Jesus had spent with them had been a teaching moment. But here they were, being told that one of them would betray Him and were left wondering—who?

Judas ended up with the short straw. But, in reality, didn't all of them ultimately betray Jesus? Yes, Judas identified Jesus to the Roman soldiers, but when the chips were down, all of them ran away in fear of facing the same fate as Jesus. Only John stood at the cross—in plain sight—with Jesus' mother, Mary.

Where do we stand? Do we run when the going gets rough? Do we stand firm in our faith? Perhaps this is a time to examine our motives. Let us stand firm, even in the face of adversity. Let us stand together; God is standing with us—His promises are true—He has promised us life abundant.

Luke 22:17, 18, 19b, 20-22 Isaiah 61:10

LEARNING FROM MISTAKES

*"I will be with him in trouble,
I will deliver him and honor him."*
Psalm 91:15b MEV

Mistakes are a part of life; however, they cannot be allowed to defeat us. As John Wesley, the founder of the Methodist tradition, says, "We are going on toward perfection." We are called to be perfect, but we haven't made it there yet—nor will we make it in this lifetime. What we must do, however, is learn from our mistakes.

A little child stumbles and falls many times before he/she learns to walk. A new-born animal stumbles along on shaky legs until it can stand. This is the way it is with the body, but even so, with the spirit. Our human nature causes us to test our limits, but God in us calls us to wait patiently for Him and He will show us the way.

God calls us to open our minds, dream our dreams, all the while walking humbly with Him. Paul learned in his quest for perfection, wholeness, and health that God's grace is sufficient to meet all his needs and that in his weakness he will be made strong by the strength of God (II Corinthians 12:9, paraphrased). So when we make our mistakes, all is not lost—ask for forgiveness and repent. Jesus said from the cross...

"Forgive them Father, for they know not what they do."
Luke 23:34

James writes,

"Count it all joy when suffering various trials." James 1:2

Trials bring us to our knees, which brings us to God, through whom comes our strength and wisdom.

Psalm 34:17-18 II Corinthians 5:7 Ephesians 3:20-21
Romans 8:6 Isaiah 10:30-31 Revelation 5:13 Isaiah 41:10

HOPE REVISITED

"God is our refuge and strength, a well-proven help in trouble." Psalm 46:1 MEV

Hope is a word that has the ability to direct a person two different ways.

(1) To those of the world, it takes on a negative—something that is only dreamed of, but can never be.
(2) But, to those who believe in the promises of God, it gives a vision of the future in which all things are beautiful, and gives you confidence.

Hope gives us an assurance that God's promises will be kept, a confidence that the bad will pass and that what is good will be persevered.

"My hope is built on nothing less than Jesus' blood and righteousness;
I dare not trust the sweetest frame, but wholly lean on Jesus' name.
On Christ, the solid Rock, I stand; All other ground is sinking sand."

(The Solid Rock; by Edward Mote & William B. Bradbury)

We can sing this hymn because we know Jesus came to show us that there is hope for a better life for all those who believe in Him. He died on the cross, taking our sins upon Himself, suffering for us, shedding His blood for us so that our burdens would be lifted—or at least made lighter. He rose, opening the door and providing a way to Heaven. That is our hope—our sure hope—that one day we will see Him face to face and sit at His feet, pouring out our love to Him. Abound in that hope.

Romans 12:12 Romans 15:13

SOMETHING ABOUT THE NAME

"...at the name of Jesus every knee should bow...and every tongue should confess that Jesus Christ is Lord..."
Philippians 2:10-11 MEV

A task lay before you. You wonder, "What have I gotten myself into?" It seems like a daunting project to bring to completion, but then you remember who has promised to be your source of strength—the Omnipotent One who sent His Son and called Him Jesus. You remember that with God all things are possible and that He has proven over and over again that He is your hope and your salvation. You can do it by allowing Christ to strengthen you! You are not alone.

The name of Jesus gives us encouragement in the midst of troubled times. The Psalmist writes that those who *"dwell in the shelter of the most high"* (Psalm 91:1) and call upon His name will be under His protection—

"He will guard you in all your ways" (Psalm 91:11).

Walking in love, giving honor and glory to God, believing in Jesus is a recipe for peace and happiness in your soul.

The task that is before you? Ask Jesus—call out His name—and if it is God's Will—nothing will stop you from accomplishing it.

Acts 4:12 Romans 8:31 Psalm 46:1-3 Luke 1:37
Philippians 4:13

RESPONSE

"Continue in prayer and be watchful with thanksgiving…"
Colossians 4:2 MEV

In my mind's eye, I'm picturing the Garden of Eden at the beginning of creation, in all its peace and beauty. Can you see it? Help us, O Lord, to get back to that peace and tranquility. Let us pray—"Blessed Holy Spirit save us from our sin."
It is true we have—as a nation—turned our backs on God. We have allowed prayer to be taken out of our schools; invocations are programmed and, in some cases, excluded altogether. "Amazing Grace," has been ordered removed from the repertoire of a marching band; to name a few incidents.

But, let us not react—instead may we respond by falling to our knees in prayer for our nation and for each of us to turn back to God and honor His Holy name in our words and deeds. The Chronicler writes,

"If My people, who are called by My name, will humble themselves and pray, and seek My face and turn from their wicked ways then I will hear from heaven, and will forgive their sin and will heal their land. Now my eyes will be open and my ears attentive to the prayer of this place."
(II Chronicles 7:14-15 MEV)

Acts 2:38 Psalm 43:10 II Peter 1:3-4

"Teach me to pray, Lord, teach me to pray/This is my heart-cry day unto day;
I long to know Thy will and Thy way/Teach me to pray, Lord, teach me to pray.
Living in Thee Lord, and Thou in me/Constantly abiding, this is my plea;
Grant me Thy power, boundless and free/Power with men and power with Thee."
("Teach Me to Pray by Albert S. Reitz, 1925; Living Hymns Hymnal)

Let every believer bow their hearts in fervent prayer—Come, Holy Spirit, lead us!

THE MAP

"And He said, 'My Presence will go with you..."
Exodus 33:14 MEV

God will show you the way.

When we are traveling in unknown territory, we consult a map, our GPS, or our Navigator App. We rely on these tools to guide us along the way. But they are not fool proof. There are incidents along the way that a map or GPS or Navigator cannot foresee. And yet, they help us on our journey.

Each and every day is a journey. We awake to a day that unfolds before us. We may think we have it all planned until a phone rings, or a knock comes on the door, or a letter in the mail—incidents that we could not foresee. How do we handle this "monkey wrench" that has been thrown into our well-laid plans?

When we know the word of God, and even more, know the Author, we are able to navigate the detours thrust in our path. Sometimes, it takes our breath away and gives us pause, but we know that God is always present as He directs our path. The writer of Proverbs puts it this way:

"A man's heart devises his way, but the Lord directs his steps." Proverbs 16:9 MEV

When traveling through traffic, hold on to His hand.

II Corinthians 1:9-10 John 15:4-7 Psalm 118:24 I Peter 2:21-22

LET ME BE EMPTY

"...and to know the love of Christ that surpasses knowledge, so that you may be filled with all the fullness of God."
Ephesians 3:19 MEV

There are many thoughts, words and actions that have the ability to fill a soul and crowd out all that is good. When one is filled with anger and bitterness and resentment, there is no room for love. Sometimes we have to decide to take out the garbage and empty ourselves.

The fact of the matter is Christ is waiting with open arms for you to come to Him—He will make you clean and give you peace. Don't let ole sloo-foot rob you of the freedom that awaits you in the arms of the Lord Jesus.

Today is a good day to be a good day. Today you can break down the bars that keep you from the freedom to love by saying "Yes" to Jesus—He will do the rest. Open your heart to Him and pray...

"Let me be full, let me be empty; I heartily yield all things to Thy disposal and pleasure." (John Wesley's Prayer)

Then you will truly be able to say with the conviction of your heart—

"This is the day the Lord has made; [I] will rejoice and be glad in it."
Psalm 118:24MEV
AMEN

Romans 8:16-17 I Samuel 16:7 I Samuel 16:17
Romans 8:38-39

TRANSFORMATION

"Come to me, all you that are weary and are carrying heavy burdens, and I will give you rest." Matthew 11:28 MEV

A new medical procedure was before me. I did not know what to expect—the doctors had told me—but hearing their words and having the actual experience are two different things.

How could I know? Would I really be safe?

My first treatment came and left me wondering even more—is this right for me? Is there something I should do to protect myself? I was tying myself up in knots! I talked to my husband and to the technicians who administered the treatment, but nothing would ease my anxiety.

Then I sat down to do my devotions—and God spoke to me through the scripture. Who else but God could lead me to the words that could set my mind at ease? He said,

"Come to me... and I will give you rest." (Matthew 11:28)

"I am with you." (Joshua 1:9)

The devotional reading reminded me that I was rehearsing trouble that might be ahead of me, instead of trusting in Jesus who will be with me guiding and directing my day. Through faith and trust in the Father, Son, and Holy Spirit, my fear was transformed into confident trust.

Yours can be, too!

Ephesians 6:10 Philippians 4:7 Matthew 14:30 Hebrews 12:2 Matthew 11:28-30
Joshua 1:5-9

BLACK FRIDAY

"When it was noon, darkness came over the whole land until three in the afternoon."
Mark 15:33 NRSV

Blackness, blood impregnate this day.

You can feel the stillness beginning to creep through-out the land.
"GET RID OF HIM! CRUCIFY HIM!" These are the shouts erupting from the crowd that stood in the midst of "the trial" that was prophecy fulfilled—though no one knew they were part of the plan.

No one knew that this terrible darkness would very soon turn into light. It would, for all those who truly believe that Jesus is the Son of God. The Roman centurion believed at the point of Jesus' death, as did the thief that was crucified next to Jesus—both received Jesus' blessing. It was a blessing filled with forgiveness—the same forgiveness that He has for you and me and all that seek forgiveness and repent of their sin.

Jesus willingly allowed Himself to be put to death; His blood flowed from His hands, His feet, and His side that you and I may be saved. Jesus, the Paschal Lamb, sacrificed Himself so now there need be no more blood sacrifices—He covers us with His blood which cleanses us of all unrighteousness.

"He [Jesus] replied, "Truly I tell you, today you will be with me in Paradise."
Luke 23:43 NRSV

May our remembrance bring us into the light!

Psalm 89:15-16 I John 1:7 Mark 15:39 Luke 23:26-49

DISRUPTIONS

"...Follow Me." John 21:19 MEV

We think we have our life all planned out and "poof!" We think we know how the medical procedure will pan out and suddenly something happens that you didn't expect. We think that raising our children is as easy as reading a book on the subject. We have disruption after disruption in the flow we think our life should take. The fact is that every disruption is a learning experience—if we view them as such, we will be fuller and more complete.

Actually, we cannot see the future or even what is going to happen tomorrow. We know where we would like our actions to take us, and perhaps, we can even envision the end result, but the area in between start and finish is uncharted waters. There is only One who can see tomorrow, all we can see is this moment. Our Lord says over and over,

*"Do not be afraid... I am with You always,
even to the end of the age."
Matthew 28:10, 20 NRSV*

When your plans are disrupted, trust in the Lord and know that it is He who is directing your path. Learn from Him—His is a far better way, the only way!

John 15:26 John 21:19 II Corinthians 4:17-18
Habakkuk 3:19

Lord, when the storms of life are raging; in the midst of tribulation; persecution, faults and failures; misunderstandings and stress; when everything seems to be falling down around me; and as I am growing old—please stand by me. Help me to see that behind every cloud is a silver lining and your light will break through. In Jesus' name, I pray. Amen

While he was still speaking, suddenly a bright cloud overshadowed them, and a voice from the cloud said, "This is My beloved Son, with whom I am well pleased. Listen to Him."
Matthew 17:5 MEV

A TRUE FIT

*"For he spoke, and it came to be;
he commanded and it stood firm."*
Psalm 33:9 NRSV

Have you ever tried to put a square peg in a round hole? It doesn't fit, no matter how you twist it or turn it. Or have you tried to put something back that came packaged in Styrofoam? It just doesn't work until you get the right combination of item and foam. You just keep trying it every which way until—"Walla! It fits!"

Our spiritual life is something like that. There is only one way it fits. We try in a myriad of ways but with no real lasting success until we get the right fit. We were created to be in a relationship with our Creator. His Spirit lives within us; we are created in their image—Father, Son, and Holy Spirit. Therefore, when we break out of that mold, or deny their existence, we just do not fit.

A true fit is when we, the believers, work in tandem with those in whose image we were created. The book of Genesis puts it this way:

"Then God said, Let US (capitals are mine) make humankind in OUR image, according to OUR likeness;" (1:26) "Be fruitful and multiply:" (1:28) "God saw everything He had made and indeed, it was very good." (1:31) NRSV

Dear Lord, I promise—with Your help—not to be a square peg in a round hole, but to honor you in all that I do and say. In Jesus' name—Amen

I Corinthians 2:10 Proverbs 2:10-12 Psalm 27:8 Philippians 4:7 Jeremiah 29:13

THE DIRECTOR

"...my word...shall accomplish that which I purpose, and succeed in the thing which I sent it." Isaiah 55:11 NRSV

Where would we be without a director?
The choir was preparing for the upcoming cantata. They were all seated in their prospective chairs. They perused their music, attempting to understand all the dynamics. If left on their own, some would interpret the score one way and others another. Some may even skip some of the most important dynamics which would make the piece come to life. They need a director!

A director knows the score. They know the beginning, the middle, and the end. A director knows the hard places and helps the choir through those places. The director knows—ahead of time—the places that could be stumbling blocks and prepares the choir.

Likewise, we need a director to help us on our journey this side of heaven. Our director is God who is *"the Alpha and the Omega—He is the beginning and the end—He IS, WAS, and ALWAYS will be"* (Revelation 1:8) *God is the one who created us.* (Genesis 1) *"He knows every hair on our head."* (Matthew 10:30)*"God directs our path."* (Proverbs 16:9)

When we are in tune and live by the beat of the Lord, we will be successful wherever we go. (Joshua 1:7)

"I pray that you may have power to comprehend, with all the saints, what is the breadth and length and depth and height, and to know the love of Christ that surpasses knowledge, so that you may be filled with the fullness of God."(Ephesians 3:18-19 MEV)

Romans 15:13 Isaiah 55:9-11 Jeremiah 29:11-12

WHO MOVED?

"...nor anything else in all creation, will be able to separate us from the love of God in Christ Jesus our Lord." Romans 8:39NRSV

Back in the day, cars were designed differently. What I'm referring to is the front seat. Back then, there was a full front seat—three people could sit side by side as the car moved down the road. Some of you may remember those "good-ole" days! A boy took his girlfriend out on a date, and they could sit close to each other as he drove. Those were the days! Then progress intruded. Now we have bucket seats, with the shifting devise, console, etc. between them.

There is a story about a husband and his wife who were out driving. Suddenly, the Mrs. Says, "Remember the days when we sat close to each other as you drove?" Mr. said, "Yes, I do, but I didn't move!"

Picture you and God in that same position. You use to be close to Him—so close that you could feel His breath and hear His heart beat. Then came a day when something intruded upon your relationship that caused you to move far away from Him, just like Mr. and Mrs. in the above vignette, it wasn't God that moved!

The fact of the matter is

"Nothing can separate you from the love of God in Christ Jesus" (Romans 8:39)—NOTHING! Jesus calls to you—

"Come follow me" (Luke 18:22) for

"My yoke is easy and my burden is light." (Matthew 11:30)

God longs for your closeness just as you long for His—He hasn't moved!

Scoot over! Sit close!

Hebrews 4:12 Deuteronomy 33:27 Romans 8:39

BE NOT ANXIOUS

"Cast all your anxiety on him, because he cares for you."
I Peter 5:7 NRSV

Jesus spoke to the people from atop the Mt. of Beatitudes, saying:

"...do not worry about tomorrow, for tomorrow will bring worries of its own. Today's trouble is enough for today."
Matthew 6:34 NRSV

He was telling the people—and us—that God will take care of them IF they trust Him and remain faithful.

It is true, we face little problems and not so little problems every day. We may face a health issue which we do not understand and do not know the outcome; our children are growing up—we wonder what will their future be like; a storm is forecast, but we do not know what affect it will have on us. God says: "Do not worry; I will take care of you." In response, we must do our research, our preparations, live a life pleasing to God—but, do not be anxious, because God has a plan and He will keep His promise to protect you and those you love.

Let Him speak to you through the Scriptures and in the place of prayer. Just as He takes care of the olive tree, the birds of the air, and the beasts in the field, He will take care of you, but even more so.

"...remember, I am with you always, to the end of the age."
Matthew 28:20b NRSV

THANK YOU, LORD.

I Corinthians 2:12 Psalm 52:8 Proverbs 3:5-6

HEAR ME

"He who is of God hears God's words." John 8:47 MEV

If your knees are knocking, kneel in prayer.

The day had started, but something just didn't seem right. My thoughts were scattered and I couldn't focus on where to start. I read the comics and completed the puzzle; I tried to relax—something wasn't right.

It soon became apparent what was wrong—I hadn't taken time to meet with the Lord. I picked up my Bible that was right at hand and had been sitting on the table waiting for me and began to read. I breathed out a sigh and breathed in the fragrance of the Spirit. Immediately, my mind began to clear and my spirit settled into a comfortable, peaceful place.

I asked the Lord, through His Holy Spirit, for His words of wisdom, love, and direction. Nothing had changed as far as what I would be facing in the day ahead, but my response would now be based upon the still, small voice of God.

Sometimes the noise of our activities can drown out the urgings of the Holy Spirit. The closer we become to God, the more we will realize that it is in the quietness of His presence that we can accomplish the most. God's still, small voice has the ability to drown out the noise and calm the storm.

Deuteronomy 31:6 I Peter 3:4 II Corinthians 4:6-7 II Corinthians 12:9

WALK WITH ME

"In the world you face persecution. But take courage; I have conquered the world!" John 16:33 NRSV

There is a spot at which we like to vacation. It is situated on the shore of the Atlantic Ocean. Once you are inside the gates of this small village, it seems as though the world doesn't exist. Our time is spent listening to music, attending worship services and Bible studies, and taking long walks along the beach. There are no sirens or traffic sounds—just the lapping of the waves and the sounds of the birds flying across the water.

When it comes time to end our time there and go back out through the gates, the world suddenly smacks us in the face! People are rushing to who knows where; cars are honking their horns because someone didn't move fast enough—suddenly the peace seems to have faded away. But, then we remember God's promises—Jesus is our peace, nothing can take that away. The Holy Spirit is walking with us through the chaos of the world—peace is always with us. It is within us.

The Psalmist writes that nothing can harm us when we walk in the shadow of the Almighty, even walking through the storm. For when we make the Lord our refuge—

"... no evil can befall [us] and no scourge come near [our] tent,(Psalm 91:10) for "those who love me I will deliver; I will protect those who know my name," (Psalm 91:14-16) says our God.

Psalm 91 Ephesians 5:7 Matthew 13:4-46 James 1:2 John 16:33

Father God, bless Your Holy Name. Father,
please help me to hear you,
To understand you, to obey you, so that my heart
is always open to you
And you alone. In Jesus' name. Amen

The Lord gives us strength to do things that we never imagined we could do. He gives us strength to face and endure when we may have wanted to quit.

I am the light of the world. Whoever follows me shall not walk in the darkness, but shall have the light of life."
John 8:12 MEV

THE LIGHTHOUSE

"Happy are those who fear the Lord...they rise in the darkness as a light to the upright;" Psalm 112:1:4 NRSV

Trouble is always with you; to hope for a time free of trouble is false hope. Our Lord tells us not to worry about tomorrow's trouble, for today has enough of its own (Matthew 6:34). The darkness is all around us—it is the light of God's love, shining through those who trust Him, that dispels it. It allows us to walk through as it shines, as does a lighthouse, to show the way. Joy, peace, and happiness surround us as we walk trusting in the Lord (Proverbs 16:20).

Troubles may be all around, but they cannot overcome you. How you respond to those troubles predicts the outcome. When troubles start to become too overwhelming, that is when you have chosen to take them on yourself. You need to come to Jesus who stands waiting for you to open the door.

"Listen! I am standing at the door knocking; if you hear my voice and open the door, I will come in and eat with you, and you with me." Revelation 3:20 NRSV

Keeping your hearts secure and firm in the Lord (Psalm 112:7) will be the light that leads you through the darkness—the darkness cannot overcome the light of Jesus Christ and His Holy Spirit who lives in you.

"Happy are those who fear the Lord...They are not afraid of evil tidings; their hearts are firm, secure in the Lord." Psalm 112:1, 7 NRSV

I Thessalonians 5:18 John 14:26 Romans 7:6 Romans 8:2 Romans 1:4-6

THE ROCK

"O Lord, my rock and my redeemer." Psalm 19:14b NRSV

Rocks have always been a part of my life, they hold a special place in my heart. Growing up on a dairy farm, there were plenty of rocks to clear away so the crops could be planted—riding on the stone boat behind a tractor is one of my fondest memories. Another is skipping stones across the water—it was not only fun, but it was an art. First, you find the smoothest, flattest stone, and then, see who could skip it the farthest. As I became older and—ahem—wiser, I grew to understand new meanings for the word rock—it moved from the physical to the spiritual part of my being.

As we grow, changes take place—these changes are sometimes difficult, but like the caterpillar who struggles to become a butterfly, the end result is beautiful. Especially in the life of the Spirit.

Living with Jesus and acknowledging that He is your rock gives you confidence and encourages you to take the next step, knowing you are not alone. Putting the rock, known as Jesus first, is the most important action in any situation. Our understandings are limited; we can only see for the moment, but Jesus' vision is complete. He will lead you on a road with less twists, turns, and detours for—

"He is the truth, the way, and the life." John 14:6 NRSV

Dear Lord, may you bless this day and teach me to lean on you for all things. No matter what I am facing, let me look at it through your eyes. AMEN.

John 4:23 John 14:1-2 Proverbs 3:5-6

INSIDE AND OUT

"O Lord, you have searched me and known me"
Psalm 139:1 NRSV

Even when you try to hide, you cannot. The little boy looked all around before putting his hand in the cookie jar—no one was in sight. In went the hand, out came the cookie—into the mouth. "No one saw me," he thinks, "I'm safe!"

This scenario can be played out many times during our lifetime in many different ways—some acts could be called less serious than others, some less hurtful or less dangerous than others, but all of them are pushing the envelope, and some are just all out sinful by anyone's standards.

We go through life committing these "little" sinful acts, thinking no one sees us. But, we are wrong! There is someone looking over our shoulder, but this "Someone" is different.

This "Someone" is watching and waiting for us to recognize Him—He is not there to condemn, but to forgive. His love for us is unconditional. It doesn't matter how many times we have put our hands in the cookie jar, thinking it was unseen, it only matters that we want a better way to live and know the One who can help us. He is the one who says:

"I am with you always, to the end of the age."
Matthew 28:20 NRSV

I John 3:6 Psalm 139:1-4

INCLINED

"I waited patiently for the Lord; he inclined to me and heard my cry."
Psalm 40:1 NRSV

Be inclined toward the Lord.

During my elementary school days, one of the happiest times was recess. The school yard was equipped with swings, slides, and see-saws. The see-saw was my favorite. A friend and I would each take an end and up and down we would go. At the bottom, I would hit the ground, but at the top, I felt free. The incline caused me to focus on my partner, watching for the push that would send me down again. One had to be ready to cushion the bump when the board came into contact with the ground.

In life, we have our ups and downs—sometimes we are up and sometimes we are down, but being watchful and ready to respond will be our salvation.

"Our help is in the name of the Lord." Psalm 124:8 NRSV

Be inclined to Him, look upon Him as a horse with blinders on; do not take your eyes off Him. He will be there for you whether you are up or down. God is with you in the valleys, as well as on the mountaintops.

"God is our refuge and strength..." Psalm 46:1 NRSV

Just utter His name—Jesus—and He will answer. Be inclined and listen with an open heart.

II Corinthians 6:17-18 Psalm 8:4-5 Genesis 1:26-27 II Corinthians 10:5 Isaiah 26:3 Psalm 146:3-4

THE PROMISE

"So we do not lose heart." II Corinthians 4:16 NRSV

I am facing some invasive oral surgery in the very near future. As the time gets closer, I'm feeling a sense of fear rising up within me. I have been told all that is going to take place and what to expect afterwards. I have been taking treatments to help me heal—everything is being done that can be done. But still, I have not experienced what I'm being told and that scares me.

Then I sat in the presence of the Lord and heard His words—

"I am with you;"
"You will face nothing alone;"
"You will get safely through each day;"
"Concentrate on today; tomorrow will take care of itself."

I breathed a sigh and released all my fears to the One who not only sees today, but all of my tomorrows. He has made me a promise that—

"[He] will never leave you nor forsake you."
(Hebrews 13:5) NRSV

I encourage you, also, to walk through today with confidence in the Living Lord who made heaven and earth and all that is within. That which He made—including you—He will protect—He will forever be before you, behind you, beside you, and within you. He loves you. *"So do not lose heart"*— have faith and walk by it.

Matthew 6:13 Romans 8:31 II Corinthians 4:18
Genesis 16:13-14

HOMESICK FOR GOD

"...the Spirit helps us in our weakness:" Romans 8:26 NRSV

Where are you? In what place physically, relationally, or spiritually do you find yourself today? The place to start is to take note of the health of your spirit— the others are a reflection of it.

Recently, I found myself in a place of exhaustion. Everything seemed to overwhelm me. The commitments I had made were becoming harder and harder to keep. I was in the middle of medical treatments to help with healing after a planned surgical procedure. My strength and stamina were slowly fading. Something had to be done!

The busyness of the daily treatments and interim doctor's visits were taking a toll. I was so busy I neglected my daily Bible reading, prayer, and meditation. I was beginning to feel I could not function—nothing mattered—until I picked up my Bible, sat in the quiet of my room, read my devotion, and had a long talk with the Lord. As I talked to Him about my (what I thought was desperate) situation and listened as He spoke to me through the meditation and His Holy Word, then, and only then, could I feel the weight lift from my soul. He will be with me through each day—something I had almost forgotten. Everything is still ahead of me—nothing in that regard has changed, but what has changed is that I know— that I know—that I **know**, God will be there, too.

"For God has not given us the spirit of fear, but of power, and love, and self-control." II Timothy 1:7 MEV

Proverbs 4:14 Romans 8:28 Psalm 42:11

DIRECTION

"I will instruct you and teach you the way you should go; I will counsel you with my eye upon you." Psalm 32:8 NRSV

Almost every woman I have spoken to lately has told me of all the things they have committed themselves to do in the day/week. They are inundated with "jobs!" They meet themselves coming and going! I wonder, are you one of them?

You are not running a race to see who can complete the most tasks! God doesn't keep a tally sheet of activities accomplished in one day. You see, eventually God **WILL** get your attention. Your bodies will call you to a halt and there will be nothing you can do, but concentrate on God's presence. You are not superwoman—she is only in the comics and movies!

Only in your communication with God may you know what He is calling you to do. He will instruct you and teach you the way you should go through the reading of His Word and meditating upon it. When you open your heart and listen, God's way will become your way.

Take an inventory of the things you do; which ones can **you** step out of; can someone else do what you are doing? Ask the Lord to lead you in your decisions. Let your no be "no" and your yes be "yes." Remember—

"Pride goes before destruction, and a haughty spirit before a fall."
Proverbs 16:18 NRSV

Luke 10:41-42 Psalm 32:8 Psalm 27:8 II Corinthians 4:7 Isaiah 12:2
Proverbs 16:9

A SHINING LIGHT

"In him was life, and the life was the light of all people."
John 1:4 NRSV

The performers were on the stage, darkness was all around them. You would not know they were even there if you didn't know the play was about to begin. Then suddenly a spot light shone on two of the performers, leaving the others still in darkness. The actors moved in and out of the spotlight as they spoke—still the rest of the stage remained in darkness.

This is very similar to our journey. We tend to move in and out of the light depending upon the circumstance and the condition of our soul. When we are in darkness, we seem to be wandering around doing and saying things that are not fulfilling to us or anyone else. But, when we are in the light, a peace that passes all understanding (Philippians 4:7) floods our soul. That is when we are walking in the spot light—the spot light of Jesus. Oh, but to walk in the spot light of Jesus' love every day!

The truth is you can! Begin your day in a "Good Morning" to the Great I Am. Read His Word and meditate upon it. Offer your day to God in prayer, inviting His Holy Spirit to direct your steps and give you His voice. You will brighten the corner where you are. We cannot ask for anything more than that!

Proverbs 29:23 Proverbs 21:2 II Thessalonians 3:13
Matthew 12:35-36 John 1:4-5
Hebrews 12:3

"But these are written that you might believe that Jesus is the Christ, the Son of God, and that believing you may have life in His name." John 20:31 MEV

THOUGHTS

"For my thoughts are not your thoughts, nor are your ways my ways, says the Lord." Isaiah 55:8 NRSV

A voice startles you and brings you back to reality. "Penny for your thoughts?" someone asked as you were deep in contemplation. Perhaps, you were enjoying a beautiful walk along a quiet stream with Jesus, and now, that walk has been interrupted. What do you say to the person who interrupted such peace? You could be rude and tell them it is none of their business. Or, you could take the opportunity to tell them the story of Jesus and the peace, joy, and love that He offers us. I pray that you would choose the latter.

When the door opens for you to witness and give testimony of your faith, you should not slam it shut. Those beautiful thoughts are from God, and God always has a plan. He knew someone was watching you, and it is He that has given you an opportunity to tell them that God loves them. **DON'T MISS IT!**

I often take the walk I spoke of in the beginning. It seems to always be leading me to an open door of a peaceful looking cabin in the woods. There is a light on and the door is open. There is someone there waiting for me, but I never quite reach the cabin—one day, though, I know that I will—by the guidance and direction of the Holy Spirit who will lead me there.

James 4:8 Matthew 1:23 Isaiah 7:14 John 1:14 Psalm 37:4
Isaiah 28:13-14
I Peter 1:8

WHATEVER

"...if there is any excellence and if there is anything worthy of praise, think on these things." Philippians 4:8 NRSV

"Whatever the day brings, I will be thankful."

Whatever is one of those words that can carry a negative or positive connotation. Used in a sentence as above, it may mean you know anything that comes your way will not get you down, because you know God is present. But, "whatever" used in response to someone confiding in you about their troubles, speaks volumes of "I don't care."

The truth is that God is always present whether we realize it or not. He wants to fulfill your life with much peace. Because of His presence, we can walk through life in the confidence that affirms our faith. When we focus on all things that are true, honorable, pure, pleasing, commendable, and anything excellent and worthy of praise—when we look for the good in every situation—then peace floods our soul.

"Whatever the day brings, I will be thankful."

Jesus speaks to us through the pages of scripture, reminding us His peace is accessible—He yearns for you to accept it.

Whatever you do, **DO NOT MISS IT!**

II Corinthians 10:5 Philippians 4:8 John 20:19:21
John 14:27

THE ROAD AHEAD

"...forgetting what lies behind and straining forward to what lies ahead."
Philippians 3:13 NRSV

God is with you even to the end of the age!
(Matthew 28:20)

Sometimes it feels as though God is not with us. Even worse, we may forget about Him! But, the truth is, no matter what we do or think, God is always with us—He is just a prayer away.

There are things that I have done in the distant past, and even in the not so distant past, that I might think could cause my relationship with God to be severed. But, you know, I have discovered there is nothing I have done that can destroy God's love for me.

God presented Himself in the flesh, called Himself Jesus, walked on this earth, suffered, bled, and died—and rose again to sit upon His throne in heaven. He took upon Himself the sins of the world—including yours and mine—and put them to death. He holds the victory over our past, present, and future sin. Nothing can separate us from the love of God.

Therefore, we—you and I—must not hold on to our past sin—lest it begins to control our words and actions. Because of what Jesus has done for us, it no longer has control over our lives, making the road ahead free of any distractions because we know our walk is being led by the love that is in Christ Jesus our Lord.

Believe—Trust—Obey

"May the God of hope fill you with all joy and peace in believing, so that you may abound in hope by the power of the Holy Spirit." Romans 15:13 NRSV

Philippians 4:7 II Timothy 1:7 Hebrews 12:2 Isaiah 41:13 Psalm 39:7

THE HEART

*"Create in me a clean heart, o God,
and put a new and right spirit within me."*
Psalm 51:10 NRSV

Fill me, O Lord, with your love.

One day a year is set aside for proclaiming, to the one most special in your life, your love—it is called Valentine's Day. You may shower that person with any number of things—flowers, candy, a special dinner, even a kiss. But, what happens the other 364/ 365 days? I would hope our words and actions every day of the year would exemplify the one day saturated with love. At least, I hope we would strive to do so, as much as it is humanly possible.

God promised Jeremiah (31:33) that days are coming when He would write the words of His love on the hearts of the people. Earlier (vs. 13) God promised to turn their mourning into joy. And later (33:3), God entreats His people to call upon Him and He will answer.

These words are not meant only for people centuries ago, they make a resounding plea to us yet today to open our hearts to the one who has shown us how to love God and one another. Paul told the Corinthians that they had written upon their hearts the spirit of the Loving Christ (II Corinthians 3:3) and it should be reflected in their words and actions.

You are the instrument through which others may know God's love for them. Allow God's love to fill your heart and then flow out to others around you—not just one day a year—but every day.

The well of Living Water will never run dry
when you live in the Spirit.

Ezekiel 36:25-27 Psalm 44:21 Psalm 34:18 Ephesians 3:20-21 Psalm 23:1-4

SLOW DOWN

"Be silent, all people, before the Lord..."
Zechariah 2:13 NRSV

We are living in a world in which everything seems to be going faster and faster. We want answers not necessarily now, but yesterday! They build cars that are said to reach speeds that wouldn't be safe on any of our roads. Our technology gives us access to anything we want to know—in record time. How does all this translate to our daily living? Do we pause for a 30 second prayer before running out the door?

"Be silent, all people, before the Lord," these were the Lord's words spoken to the exiles through the prophet Zechariah. God's people had been exiled due to their lack of obedience to the Lord. However, even in exile, God never left them and now He is calling them to return to their lives as His obedient and faithful children. He calls them to stop running away.

Many times, we find ourselves in the very same situation. We are running so fast and thinking it all depends upon us that we neglect to open our hearts to the One who loves us unconditionally. Sometimes we, too, will find ourselves in a similar exile. But, even so, God, Jesus, and the Holy Spirit are only a prayer away.

Consider making that call—as God's word in Jeremiah says:

"Call to me and I will answer you, and I will tell you great and hidden things that you have not known." (33:3) NRSV

Isaiah 40:31 Zechariah 2:13 Isaiah 30:15 II Corinthians 12:9

RESTORATION

"For I will restore health to you; and your wounds I will heal, says the Lord." Jeremiah 30:17 NRSV

The Lord spoke to Jeremiah concerning Israel and Judah—it was not a message of gloom, but of salvation. God was promising to restore His people to freedom and prosperity. They had fallen and suffered at the hands of their captors, but God had heard their cries. They will return and serve the Lord their God.

Many times, we cry out in pain and suffering. We wonder, "Where is God?"

Does He not care?"
Has He closed His ears to me?"

There is a reason that we are left in our sufferings but, never fear, God is there with you—waiting for you to call out to Him and tell Him you love Him.

The word that came to Jeremiah is the same word that comes to you

"I will restore health to you; and your wounds I will heal."
(Jeremiah 30:17) NRSV

And just as the angel said to the women at the tomb, He says to you:

"Do not be afraid" (Matthew 28:5). NRSV

God reassures you,

"I will never leave you or forsake you." (Hebrews 13:5) NRSV

Don't miss the Lord's reaching out to you; come to Him, open your heart—don't let pride (Proverbs 16:18) keep you from the greatest blessing you will ever receive.

Jesus says,

"I am the way, and the truth, and the life." John 14:6 NRSV

Ephesians 5:8 Romans 5:3-4 Jeremiah 30:7 Matthew 28:5-7 II Corinthians 5:17

AWAKEN

*"My soul waits for the Lord more than
those who watch for the morning."*
Psalm 130:6 NRSV

**God holds your right hand; He will never let go.
(Psalm 73:23)**

You awaken from a dream just before you complete a fall—you awaken before your ultimate death, or at the very least, terrible injuries. Those who interpret dreams might say something dreadful is about to happen, but do not worry, you will find your way out—that is the worldly view. Others, speaking in the spiritual sense, would tell you that God will not let you fall; have faith and trust Him in all your ways.

A fall, in any sense of the word, is frightening. But your fall can be cushioned by recognizing that God will take care of you. Sometimes falls are necessary to get your attention. There is something you must learn or change. As is said, "Drastic situations take drastic actions."

Do not fear, *"the Lord, your God is in your midst, a warrior who gives victory; he will rejoice over you with gladness he will renew you with his love; he will exult over you with loud singing as on a day of festival." Zephaniah 3:17 NRSV*

Whatever battle, circumstance, or situation you are in, God has already won the victory. Awaken, open your eyes, and allow Him into your heart.

Ephesians 5:14 Psalm 130:5-6 Psalm 138:8 Psalm 73:23-26

WAITING FOR HOPE

"Be of good courage, and He shall strengthen your heart, all you who hope in the Lord." Psalm 31:24 NKJV

God, the Lord, is my strength, in Him I will trust. My hope is in the Lord.

Living in hope is what can get us through a difficult time. Hope is birthed through our faith that God holds us in the palm of His hand and will never leave us. Hope is what helps us to understand that God loved us long before we were born. He loves us even in the midst of our sin and calls us back to walk in righteousness, not once, but over and over again.

Whatever troubles you are going through—be it financial, physical, relational, or spiritual—hope will lead you through to victory. If you do not have hope now, wait for it, have courage—be encouraged—reach out to God through His Son, Jesus Christ. Pour out your heart to Him and feel His love flow into your being. He is but a breath away. He is waiting for you with His arms out-stretched.

God watches out for and protects all His creations—exult Him and give Him thanks and He will act on your behalf.

Wait upon and put your hope in the Lord—be of good courage.

*"May he grant you your heart's desire,
and fulfill all your plans."
Psalm 20:4 NRSV*

Proverbs 18:10 Exodus 3:14 Habakkuk 3:17-19

THE HOPE OF GLORY

*"...God chose to make known...
the riches of the glory of the mystery..."*
Colossians 1:27 NRSV

"Now faith is the assurance of things HOPED for, the conviction of things not seen." Hebrews 11:1

Struggling to find our niche in life can be devastating—especially for young people. It may seem that everything you try knocks you down. But you keep getting up and try again. Good for you!! It may seem that you have tried everything to reach your goal. Perhaps, the dollar signs have clouded your vision. You know, the new car, the house, the travel, the beautiful girl or handsome man on your arm. I want to tell you, all this is non-consequential—it is not what success is really all about.

Perhaps there is one thing that hasn't been tried. There is a mystery that you haven't solved yet. But now you might be ready. The mystery is really the meaning of all life—it is the essence of life—without which there can be no peace.

If you will seek God's face and turn from wanting to do your own will, God will hear your prayer and heal you (II Chronicles 7:14). Admit that you can do nothing on your own (John 5:30) and Jesus will give you the peace that passes all understanding (John 14:27). That, my friend, is **the hope of glory**.

Jeremiah 33:3 Jeremiah 1:8-9 Colossians 1:27
Colossians 3:15 Ephesians 1:17-18

OLD AGE

"They shall still bear fruit in old age; they shall be filled with vitality and foliage." Psalm 92:14 *MEV*

Antiques increase in value as they age. Wine is better and tastes better when it is aged.

Grandma Moses began her marvelous painting career at the age of 78. The author of "To Kill a Mocking Bird," Harper Lee, lived a long life, and still after her death, at age 89, another manuscript was found and published. Age, chronologically speaking, can be a deterrent, but age, as a matter of mind, is the key to living joyfully.

Leaning on Jesus, coming to God in prayer through Him, settles the soul and gives us peace. The hairs of the head may get gray or thin a bit, but the growth of the spirit is paramount to a long, happy, peaceful life. There is much to do and God will continue to use you. There are still mountains to climb and treasures to be discovered. Who knows what will be in store if you depend upon God to show you the way. Nothing is too small or too old in the eyes of the Lord.

Paul writes, *"...with God all things are possible."* (Matthew 19:26) MEV

May your prayer be,
"I can do all things because of Christ who strengthens me." Philippians 4:13 MEV

Psalm 16:8 Psalm 40:2 Colossians 4:2 I Thessalonians 5:18-19

SECRET THINGS

"The secret things belong to the Lord our God..."
Deuteronomy 29:29 MEV

WHERE THERE SEEMS TO BE NO WAY, GOD WILL MAKE A WAY.

What energy it takes to plan and try to figure out what is going to happen tomorrow! A plan is in place, but it doesn't always work out. And we say, "If I had only known—if I had only seen—I could've done such-n-such!"

Solomon, in all his wisdom, told us centuries ago:

"The human mind plans the way, but the Lord directs the steps." Proverbs 16:9 NRSV

God will reveal to you what you need to know when the time is right. Jesus spoke to the people on the Mount of Beatitudes and told them not to worry about tomorrow... he told them not worry, because he would take care of them as he does the birds of the air and the fish of the sea. (Matthew 6:25-34)

Worrying cannot add a single moment to your life; in fact, it does just the opposite.

The things of the future are only for God to know. They are kept a secret for the time being, but at the right time, they will be revealed. **Meanwhile,** trust and walk with God.

Ecclesiastes 4:9-10 Psalm 32:8 Psalm 16:11

WITHIN THE BOUNDARIES

"Enter through the narrow gate...For the gate is narrow and the road is hard that leads to life..." Matthew 7:13-14 NRSV

There is nowhere in the scriptures that says following the path that God has laid out for you will be easy. In fact, wanting things to be easy is why many do not enter the gates of heaven. Just as peace is not the absence of conflict, it is also true that success and happiness is not spelled E A S Y.

Therefore, it is a hard task to make the right choice. Faced with a situation that involves spending hard-earned money to achieve a goal or not spending the money and having to find a new way is very perplexing and stressful. Which is right? Which is the narrow door? God knows.

Sometimes it is hard to hear God's voice when the excitement of meeting the goal seems to drown out everything else. But, then again, could it be God showing the way that He has planned? He speaks,

"[I] make known to you the path of life; in [My] presence there is fullness of joy; at [My] right hand there are pleasures for evermore.." (Psalm 16:11) MEV

I pray, O Lord that my eyes will be opened; my spirit quieted; and the path made clear.

AMEN

Malachi 3:18 Psalm 16:11 I Corinthians 10:13

HOLD ON TIGHT

"Do not worry about anything, but in everything by prayer and supplication with thanksgiving, let your requests be made known to God." Philippians 4:6 NRSV

Hold on tight, you are in for the ride of your life!

This is what we should be taught as soon as we are old enough to understand. The seconds, minutes, hours, days, weeks, months, and years ahead will be filled with all sorts of situations that will either knock us down or lift us up. And the fact of the matter is we may not know which is which until after the fact.

Our salvation can only be held in the hands of God. He, and He alone, can know the future, for He has planned it—our job is to have faith, depend on His Word, and spend time with Jesus that we may know Him.

We cannot lean on our own understanding, for our understanding has limits. Rather, we need to depend upon God who directs our path and always works for our good. If we do happen to stumble, God promises to lift us up again when we call out to Him. Living for Jesus gives us peace and pleasures beyond measure—even our sorrows turn into joy because our character has been strengthened.

BLESS ME, O LORD, THIS DAY.

Affirm your trust in the Lord; wait hopefully in His Presence and watch to see what He will do.

Proverbs 10:22 Philippians 4:19 Isaiah 26:3 John 11:25
Matthew 11:28-29
I Peter 1:8-9

TRUST ME

"...I will wait for the God of my salvation." Micah 7:7 NRSV

"Trust and Obey," we sing, "for there is no other way."

How can we know the right way to turn? Where can we find counsel that is not corrupted with their own self interests? It is like walking through the woods in the dark of the night. There is darkness all around; all you can do is feel your way through. Then, suddenly, you see a glimmer of light and direct your steps toward it. That light is your salvation.

When facing dark, uncharted times in your life, you must search for the light. If you do not see it at first, wait and trust; it will appear. Things may seem dark and hopeless at the moment, but God is there waiting for you to ask Him for help—when you do, He will answer.

Turn your hopelessness into hope—your darkness into light.

"For in hope we are saved." (Romans 8:24) NRSV

And
"Rejoice in hope, be patient in suffering, persevere in prayer" (Romans 12:12) NRSV

And most of all,
"Trust in the Lord with all your heart, and do not rely on your own insight." (Proverbs 3:5) NRSV

"And now, O Lord, what do I wait for? My hope is in You. Deliver me from all my transgressions." (Psalm 39:7-8) NRSV

James 4:2-3 Isaiah 40:31 Micah 7:7 Ephesians 4:1-6
John 10:4

OPEN THE GATES

*"Open the gates that the righteous nation
which keeps the faith may enter in."*
Isaiah 26:2 NRSV

Sometimes it becomes necessary to open the gates that water may be released from the reservoir into the channel. Sometimes our days become full to the point of overflowing with activities that we feel like we are drowning. We need to come up for air and float peacefully on our backs for a while.

In previous years, it has been reported that due to the humongous amount of rainfall, rivers were overflowing their banks and invading people's homes and roadways. This drastic situation called for a drastic response. People had to flee their homes to safety.

In life, we run into floods of circumstances such as—illness; marital problems; job loss; difficulties with our children; drugs and alcohol addictions—all of which call for drastic action that will save our life or the lives of those we love.

At those times, you need to open the flood gates, not to let something out, but to let something in—the love of Jesus Christ. Focusing on the problem only gives the problem leverage, but focusing on Christ's love for you, gives you a positive perspective, and helps you through. When you see Jesus, the darkness in your life fades in the light of His love.

II Chronicles 7:14 Isaiah 26:2-3 Psalm 143:8 Luke 12:25-26
I Thessalonians 5:16-18

FRIENDS

"We know that all things work together for good for those who love God, who are called according to his purpose."
Romans 8:28 NRSV

MAKE FRIENDS WITH YOUR ENEMIES!

You have a choice how you respond to the actions of those who seek to hurt you. Bullies relish the fact that the one whom they are bullying succumbs to fear. Fear is your enemy, and the bully feeds on it.

However, when you stand up to the face of fear, it immediately dissipates, and the bully's ego is deflated. Jesus said, *"Love your enemies and pray for those who persecute you."* (Matthew 5:44)

Hard? Of course, but there is nothing in God's Word that says it will be easy! Jesus didn't say to become buddies; just do not return offenses with angry or vengeful words and actions—that plays right into the bully's' hand and gives them power they haven't earned.

Ask the Lord to help you—speak with Him with sincerity of heart and make Him your friend. Paul spoke to the church at Philippi, saying,

"My God shall supply your every need according to His riches in glory by Christ Jesus." (Philippians 4:19) MEV

And the Psalmist chimes in-

"When I am afraid, I put my trust in [God]."
(Psalm 56:3) NRSV

MAKE THIS YOUR MANTRA

Galatians 6:2 John 16:23-24 1 Corinthians 1:23-24

WORSHIP AND PRAISE

*"But the Lord is in his holy temple:
let all the earth keep silence before him!"
Habakkuk 2:20 NRSV*

A special day

On the Sabbath houses of worship all around the world are welcoming pilgrims as they come to worship and praise the One who has given them life. Regardless of what may be occurring in their lives, they know as believers that they are not alone and their God will make a way if they trust Him.

In these houses of worship, there is someone who will give an inspirational message that has been prepared through prayer. Let us take a moment to offer a prayer to Almighty God that the message will reach the open hearts of the people who have gathered. Let us ask God to fill the messenger with His Holy Spirit and make them on fire for the Lord.

There is no other place to be on the Sabbath. The writer of Hebrews tells us to,

"Not neglect to meet together; (Hebrews 10:25) NRSV

It is of great encouragement to be with those of like minds and hearts. All of us are experiencing our own trials and tribulations and each may receive encouragement to take another step and face another day because we have been reminded that He lives!

SEE YOU AT WORSHIP

I Timothy 2:1-3 Hebrews 11:13 Ephesians 2:19 I John 1:7
Hebrews 7:25
Psalm 37:3-4

THE HELPER

*"Our help is in the name of the Lord,
who made heaven and earth."*
Psalm 124:8 NRSV

Those who are in the dead of winter, may wonder, "When will this be over?" The snow and cold seem to be caving in on you—there seems to be no end to the long cold nights and shortened days. You are impatient even though you know that spring is coming; after all, you've been here before.

Life is full of impatient moments and time doesn't always seem to be on our side. An illness, a job completed, children to mature, writing to be recognized—there are any number of things that are held in the hands of time and the One who created all things. But, we have a Helper.

"Our help is in the name of the Lord, who made heaven and earth" (Psalm 124:8) whose Holy Spirit lives within us. If God's Holy Spirit lives within us, and we believe that He does, is there anything that can harm us?

GOD WILL NOT LET HIMSELF BE DESTROYED!

Just as the winter gives way to the spring, so too, whatever is happening in your life will give way to victory. Trust in God and know that the struggle you are experiencing is strengthening you—even at this moment. <u>God will take care of you—in His Time.</u>

Mark 9:23 Philippians 1:6 Psalm 62:8 Psalm 63:7-8
James 1:2-4

HOLD MY HAND

"...though we stumble, we shall not fall headlong, for the Lord holds us by the hand."
Psalm 37:24 NRSV

Teach me to walk in Thy way, O Lord.

When a little child is learning to stand, then to walk, there are many falls. But, someone is always there to cushion that fall. Remembering our days, or the days that our children, were learning to walk, helps us to understand how much more the Lord God protects our stumbling ways. If we can love our children enough to protect them from the falls they take, how much more will our Heavenly Father protect us, as He loves us unconditionally?!?

As we mature spiritually and learn to walk following the steps of Jesus, we too will stumble. God calls to us, saying, "Hold my hand, my child; I will keep you from falling." We might trip or stub our toe, but the Lord will keep us from falling headlong, for He holds us by the hand. All who believe have this promise!

In a dream, you may see yourself falling from a roof-top, but you awaken before you hit the ground. Who do you think has awakened you? Who keeps you from hitting the ground? Turn to Psalm 91 in your Bible and you will find the answer.

Psalm 37:23-24 Psalm 18:30 Psalm 91:11-14

IN HIS TIME

*"For everything there is a season,
and a time for every matter under heaven."*
Ecclesiastes 3:1 NRSV

YOU MAKE ALL THINGS BEAUTIFUL IN YOUR TIME, LORD.

We are living in a time where everything is instant. We want everything the fastest way that it could possibly be accomplished. Waiting is becoming a bad word in our modern culture. The impatience of the world is going to be its downfall, unless a halt is called. Take a moment to take a breath; to smell the roses; to spend time with your children; and to have a conversation with your spouse or a friend—OR SAY A PRAYER.

The truth is, God cannot be rushed. He has a plan, and that plan is the best!

In His time, He will make all things beautiful. Take your time to experience all the beauty and joy and love that He has planned for you. Don't be so busy that you miss it!

"This is the day the Lord has made, rejoice and be glad in it."
(Psalm 118:24) NRSV

Tomorrow will take care of itself.

Holy Spirit, teach me to wait upon the Lord. Help me to persevere in lifting my needs to you, though I may not see an answer immediately. Help me to trust that You know my needs even better than I. Trusting in you is the only way to know peace and happiness—which turns into joy. In Jesus' name, Amen.

Psalm 32:7 II Corinthians 5:7 Galatians 5:25 Luke 18:1

BE TRANSFORMED

"The Lord has said to me, "My grace is sufficient for you, for power is perfected in weakness." II Corinthians 12:9 (NASB)

DO NOT BE ASHAMED OF YOUR WEAKNESSES, BOAST ABOUT THEM!

It is so hard to wrap your mind around the phrase, "when I am weak, I am strong." How can one be weak and strong at the same time? All our lives we are told in one way or another to be strong. You fall when you are little, and someone tells you, "It's *OK*, get up and keep going." In school, you goof at something, get a poor mark, or strike out in the softball game, or lose your boyfriend/girlfriend, and you hear one way or another, "Hold your head up, put your shoulders back, and be strong—be tough." It has been ingrained in us to be strong. But, God says your weaknesses are not to be hidden!

You see, it is in His strength that we must walk; when we admit those weaknesses, acknowledging that we cannot succeed on our own, that is when God steps in and shows us the way. He then is able to transform our minds. He hears us and helps us to rise above the criticism of the world. Only in the transformation of your life will God give you understanding and quiet your soul.

Take a moment—breathe out all that constrains you—breathe in and be filled with God's precious Holy Spirit. *"Be still and know that I am God!" (Psalm 46:10)*

Colossians 2:6-7 Colossians 1:10 Romans 6:4 *Psalm 101:2* II Corinthians 3:18
Ephesians 3:17

WORDS

"Pleasant words are like a honeycomb, sweetness to the soul and health to the body."
Proverbs 16:24 NRSV

ONCE THE WORDS ARE SAID YOU CANNOT TAKE THEM BACK!

There is an old adage that we use to say—it goes like this: "Sticks and stones may break my bones, but words will never hurt me." NOT TRUE! It sounded good at the time and it kept the name calling and jeering at bay for a while, BUT there is no doubt it hurt with a hurt that sometimes wouldn't heal as a broken bone would. There are people whose lives have been ruined by the words that have been said to them.

There is help for the people who feel that they are empowered by the mean and nasty words they say, as well as for the ones who hear them. That help comes from the Word of God. God's word speaks of the love He has for you through His Son, Christ Jesus, who died that you might live life abundantly with joy.

Listening to positive messages of the abundance of God's love for you and reading His Word is healing for your heart; for out of your heart the words of your mouth are formed. Harsh words are spoken out of an aching heart.

Call out to God; ask Him to cleanse you of all unrighteousness. God has plans for you, plans of welfare and hope.

Matthew 12:34 Psalm 17:3 Psalm 19:14 Philippines 4:13
Proverbs 17:22
Jeremiah 29:11-12

DOUBT

"...ask in faith, never doubting" James 1:6 NRSV

Standing on the beach watching the waves roll in and roll out, one is embraced by the power of God. As far as the eye can see there is nothing but water. Suddenly, you feel at one with all of creation. The birds are skimming the water for food and the little sandpipers are running back and forth at the water's edge, grabbing their food as it washes ashore. All nature seems to be in harmony, and you are a part of it. It is at times like these when all doubt is erased from your mind. You feel the power of God, who is in charge of the universe and everything in it.

Now, consider the rolling in and out of the waves. The rolling in of the waves represent the times in your life when you are walking in faith, when the times of indecision and doubt are kept at bay. It brings you closer to God where you can bask in His love. Then consider the waves as they roll out, pulling everything with them. This represents the times that you doubt your decisions and wonder where God is. Everything seems to be slipping from your grasp.

Walking in faith keeps those times of indecision and doubt at bay. It closes the gap and doesn't allow Satan to work his discontent or plant any doubt in your mind. Having faith in God calls to reason all that is good and right and pure.

"Delight yourself in the Lord, and He will give you the desires of your heart."
Psalm 37:4 NRSV

James 1:2-4; 6-8 Mark 11:22-24

GETTING RID OF TANGLES

"The Lord God said to the woman, "What is this you have done?" the woman said, "The serpent deceived me, and I ate." Genesis 3:13MEV

When I was young, I had tight, curly, red hair. Each day, my mother would brush and comb out all the tangles. I remember how much it hurt—it was not something I looked forward to, but it was necessary to get rid of them, or they would only get worse.

Sometimes we have to get rid of the tangles in our lives—if we do not, we might find ourselves up to our necks in hot water. The saying goes, "Oh, what a tangled web we weave, when we practice to deceive." Eve found herself in that tangled web. She owned up to eating the forbidden fruit, but in the process, she blamed it on the serpent. Actually, she did not take full responsibility—she shouldn't have listened.

The serpent represents those who do not follow God and think they are above Him. They are the ones who believers must not listen to. They speak with flowery words; they speak with many words; they paint a picture that seems too good to be true—and it is!

Before responding to such a person, pause giving the Holy Spirit space to act through you. We need to keep the tangles out to avoid the pain and heartache of removing them once they are there. Instead, let us commit to walking in the smoothness of day to day living with God through prayer, reading His Word, and listening to Him.

Psalm 119:63 Proverbs 27:17 Proverbs 12:26
Colossians 6:19

DENYING THE GIFT

"...the fruit of the spirit is love, joy, peace, patience, kindness, generosity, faithfulness, gentleness, and self-control." Galatians 5:22-23 NRSV

MELT ME, MOLD ME, FILL ME, USE ME

The doorbell rang. Who could that be? I'm not expecting anyone! As I opened the door, I saw a delivery person holding a package in his hands. I affirmed that I was the person to whom it was addressed and took the package. But who could this be from? And what could it be? It's not my birthday or any other special day!

Upon opening the package, I found a card which said, "This gift is to remind you of how special you are—please use it to bring glory to God who has called you."—signed "a friend." It was a Bible!

As I pondered what had just happened, I began to realize that the precious gifts that had been given to me by God and His Holy Spirit who lives within me were not being used—I was turning my back on the most precious gifts that could ever be given to me. And, not only that, I was grieving the one who had given them to me by denying Him.

God's Word, the Holy Bible, is essential reading to understand God's Will for your life. He speaks to you through His Word—ask the Holy Spirit to open the eyes of your heart so that you may delight in all the gifts He has given you.

I Corinthians 3:1-17 Psalm 36:7-9 Psalm 132:15
John 6:12-13

MY PRAYER

"May the Lord direct your hearts to the love of God and to the steadfastness of Christ." II Thessalonians 3:5 NRSV

Paul wrote a letter of encouragement to the church (a group of believers) at Ephesus. Paul wrote to encourage them to keep the faith. They had risen from death into life by turning their backs on the evil that had had control over them. Paul had encouraged them in a far better way—the way of Christ—the way of love, not hate.

In the same way, we need encouragement to stay the course. There are so many darts being thrown our way in the form of temptations that seem good. They seem too good to be true—and they are. Alcohol, drugs, sex give us a high, but it only lasts for a while. When we come down, it is with a bang!

We are the temple of the Holy Spirit who offers us peace. He does not say it will be easy, but he does say the reward will be great.

This is Paul's prayer for the Ephesians AND for us:

"I pray that the God of our Lord Jesus Christ, the Father of glory, may give you a spirit of wisdom and revelation as you come to know him, so that, with the eyes of your heart enlightened, you may know what is the hope to which he has called you, what are the riches of his glorious inheritance among the saints and what is the immeasurable greatness of his power for us who believe according to the working of his great power."

Ephesians 1:17-19 NRSV
This is my prayer. AMEN

Isaiah 59:19 Ephesians 6:10-20 II Corinthians 10:4-5 II Timothy 4:18

RECEPTION

"As you therefore have received Christ Jesus the Lord, continue to live your lives in him," Colossians 2:6 NRS

My family bought their first television set when I was about ten years old—around 1948. We didn't have cable or a dish for our reception, but we did have an antenna. It was erected in the ground behind our house that was situated on a high point of the property. There were days that the reception was clear and days when it was "snowy." In order to have good reception, the antenna had to be pointed in the right direction. Sometimes the wind was so strong that it changed the position of the antenna and Dad would have to go out and re-adjust it.

The same is true of our reception of Christ Jesus in our lives. Our antenna must be pointed in the right direction for the reception to be clear. Adjusting our antenna by reading God's Word, prayer, and surrounding ourselves with people who are Christ-minded keeps our reception clear.

Sometimes a big gust of wind may threaten the reception of the love of God. This may come in the form of temptation. When we are in a weakened state because of lack of rest, a poor diet, or too much stress, temptation presents itself as an easy way to live. But, believe me, it is a wolf in sheep's clothing and soon will devour you. Perfect reception comes when you,

"Trust in the Lord...for in Him you have an everlasting rock."
  Isaiah 26:4 NRSV

Romans 12:11 John 16:8 Philippians 2:17

THE TIME IS NEAR

"...put on the Lord Jesus Christ, and make no revision for the flesh, to gratify its desires." Romans 13:14 NRSV

The day is drawing near. The Lord soon will be making His appearance once again. However, there is no need to fear the erupting violence we see in the world.

"Do not be afraid of them, for I am with you to deliver you, says the Lord."
Jeremiah 1:8 NRSV

Hold fast to your belief and never stop trusting in the Lord—His promises are true—He will come and save you. Remain steady in your prayers, in your solitude, and with one another.

The Gospels, Paul, Peter, and the writer of Hebrews all address the chaos that will be in the days before the Lord appears—not to mention John's writing in the book of Revelation. Old Testament writers also addressed the end times—Isaiah, Jeremiah, the Psalmists.

There are 365 passages placed through-out the Bible that tell us in one way or another—DO NOT BE AFRAID! It seems it is significant to our lives! What we need to do is keep on loving, for in that way, we are keeping the commandments and showing our faith and hope in the Lord God.

"You, O Lord, will protect us;" Psalm 12:7 NRSV

Immerse yourself in prayer and the reading of His Word, and the Evil One cannot come near you or yours.

I Peter 4:7 Matthew 24:13 Romans 13:11 II Peter *3:9*

I lift up my eyes to the hills—from where will my help come?
My help comes from the Lord, who made heaven and earth.
He will not let your foot be moved; he who
keeps will not slumber.
He who keeps Israel will neither slumber nor sleep.
The Lord is your keeper; the Lord is your shade at
your right hand.
The sun shall not strike you by day, or the moon by night.
The Lord will keep you from all evil; he will keep your life.
The Lord will keep your going out and your coming in
from this time on and forevermore.
Psalm 121 NRSV

"Embracing the Call"(Rev. Betty's first book) is the story of a life split in two by a day of reckoning that changed one woman's path in life and created a legacy that has touched three generations. And it is the tale of a shining example of what can happen when you stop guessing, say "yes" to God, and discover your own divine call.

CPSIA information can be obtained
at www.ICGtesting.com
Printed in the USA
LVOW06s0856020816
498359LV00005B/8/P